Ship Handling
in
Narrow Channels

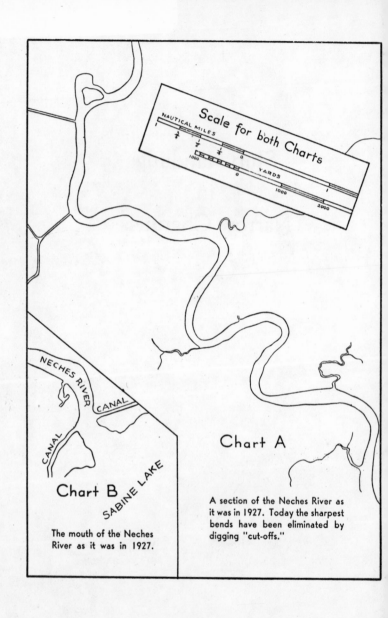

Scale for both Charts

NAUTICAL MILES

1000

YARDS

1000

2000

Chart A

A section of the Neches River as it was in 1927. Today the sharpest bends have been eliminated by digging "cut-offs."

Chart B

The mouth of the Neches River as it was in 1927.

NECHES RIVER

CANAL

CANAL

SABINE LAKE

SHIP HANDLING in NARROW CHANNELS

Enlarged Third Edition

CARLYLE J. PLUMMER
Sabine Pilots (Ret.)

CORNELL MARITIME PRESS, INC.
Cambridge   Maryland
1978

Library of Congress Cataloging in Publication Data

Plummer, Carlyle J
  Ship handling in narrow channels.

  1. Ship handling.   2. Inland navigation.
I. Title.
VK545.P5   1978   623.89'0916'93   78-15384
ISBN 0—87033—247-3

Because he has been a help and
inspiration to me throughout
my seafaring career,
this book is dedicated to

THOMAS FENLON

Master Mariner

The S/S Manhattan *is the largest merchant vessel ever to be built in the United States, as well as one of the largest vessels in the world; her length is 940' and her beam is 132' 6". She is shown approaching a bascule bridge whose opening is "tight" for her.*

Acknowledgments

The author is indebted to several persons and organizations for help given him in finding illustrative and background material. He particularly wishes to express his appreciation to Captain G. R. Holmes, Mr. T. T. Hunt, and Mr. E. M. Black; also to the Beaumont Chamber of Commerce and D. M. Picton & Co.

Manhattan photographs in the Revised Edition are through the courtesy of Gordon E. Baxter Jr., Correspondent, Radio Station KTRM, Beaumont, Texas.

The S/S Manhattan *is "squeezing" through the opening. The proximity of the ship to her port bank—aggravated by the great distance from her starboard bank—causes suction to be very strong only on her port quarter. Therefore, special allowance and precaution must be taken in order to cope with suction's harmful effects.*

Foreword

There is some information a commanding officer should have that cannot be found in texts. Under normal conditions, when promotion is slow, this knowledge is acquired—to a sufficient degree—by "absorption."

However, with promotion as rapid as it is today, there is a likelihood that some of the knowledge that ordinarily is simply "handed down" may be lost. SHIP HANDLING IN NARROW CHANNELS points out some essential facts that a man might normally witness only at rare intervals in long service as a junior officer, and which he might therefore never encounter during his service as a subordinate today, when promotion is rapid.

Until recent years many waterways were so narrow, crooked and shallow that they could be successfully navigated only by completely utilizing every advantage.

Today these waterways have been widened, straightened and deepened, thus minimizing these problems.

Therefore, being familiar with how to take the utmost advantage of a condition such as suction is apt to become a lost art that requires relearning. It needs to be relearned because ships like the *Manhattan* and her many sisters that are sure to follow have caused these improved waterways to again become narrow, crooked and shallow.

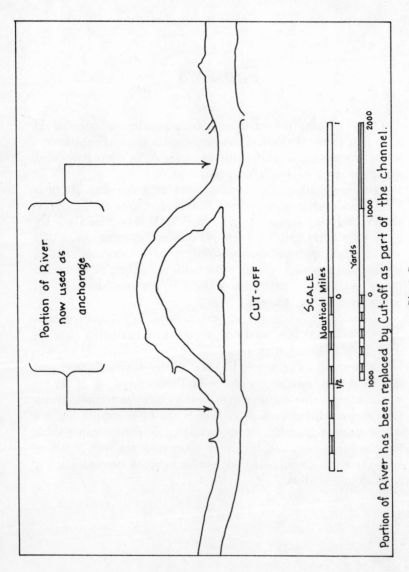

Portion of River now used as anchorage

CUT-OFF

SCALE

Nautical Miles

Yards

Portion of River has been replaced by Cut-off as part of the channel.

Chart C

Contents

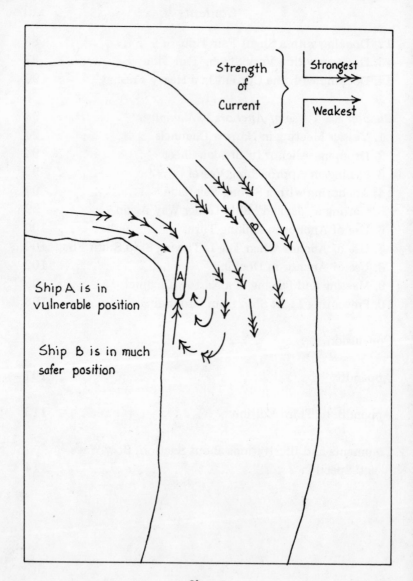

Chart D

Illustrations

Sketches of Portions of The Sabine District Waterways

Ship Handling
in
Narrow Channels

Chapter One

Making Suction an Asset

1. SUCTION IN CONFINED WATERS

Whenever vessels navigate inland waters, suction is apt to have some effect on their handling. However, except when the channel is narrow and shallow, in relation to the size and draft of the vessel, suction may be, and generally is, disregarded without the vessel getting out of control. But once in a while, when navigating in confined waters, a ship[1] is likely to become unmanageable simply because the officer in charge fails to anticipate and guard against the effects of suction. Furthermore, the increased size and speed of present day ships has made it important to give more consideration than in the past to the ill-effects ships may cause —through suction—when passing other vessels.

Therefore, anything which can be a valuable asset, but which *is* a source of danger and trouble if not properly understood and allowed for, should be well worth consideration.

Suction, in this book, will be referred to in its broadest sense, as including all the various disturbances—with one exception— that are caused by any type of craft when she is under way, or when for any other reason (such as being aground, moored or anchored) the water passes by her. The exception is this: When

[1] Throughout the narration (unless otherwise stated or shown) whenever size, speed, etc., need to be specified, it will be assumed the *ship* is an average, modern—well-deck, right-handed, single-screw—freighter or tanker 500 feet long, with other dimensions in proportion.

the surface waves that trail off on each side have gone beyond the immediate vicinity of the craft, then they are no longer thought of as suction.

At the risk of being adjudged grossly superstitious, the assertion will be made that vessels seem to have life, because there is evidence that they are capable of fear. They are afraid of shoal water, and that fear is expressed through suction. The reader is asked to accept this theory—when the explanations require it—during the course of this narration.

Ships not only seem to have life, but in some cases seem positively human. Though speechless, they very emphatically are not dumb, because they most certainly are capable of imparting vital information. Like people, ships can be put into two broad classifications. Some ships seem excitable and entirely unreliable in times of stress; others seem coolheaded and dependable even under the most trying conditions. For example, just as some people become panicky when confronted with danger, some ships, when they get close to a shoal, "go wild" and get completely out of control. Other ships, although they also unmistakably signify their dread of shoal water, can—if properly understood and handled—be induced to stay close to it. So it behooves the master, or whoever is doing the handling or piloting, to become as thoroughly acquainted as possible with the meaning of his vessel's actions.

As evidence that a dependable ship can cooperate and converse intelligibly with her master, consider this instance: Assume that a ship is running in a straight but narrow channel with shoal water on both sides, and for some reason, such as fog or darkness, the location of the channel cannot be discerned. Then in the event she should get too close to either bank—if she is a dependable ship— she will calmly inform her master of this fact by carrying extra rudder toward the shoal water. If it is necessary to keep her close to the bank, she can be made to stay there, in spite of the fact that she would prefer not to do so. On the other hand, if it is desired to keep the center of the channel, this can be accomplished through heeding her warning by altering the course slightly—say, one or two degrees. The ship will signify when she has gotten a little farther away from the bank by carrying less rudder, and will indicate when she has reached the center of the channel by ceasing entirely to carry extra rudder.

2. CUTTING THE POINT

Thus we may see how a ship conveys information that is extremely helpful in keeping her in a straight reach of a channel. Now let us consider how she tells when she has come to a bend, and how, by understanding the meaning of her actions—and frequently in no other way—the bend can be negotiated.

Assume the officer in command knows he is approaching a bend where the direction of the channel gradually changes from, say, North to East. He must have some unmistakable means of knowing positively when the bend has been reached. The lead will be of little or no help because the bank shoals up too abruptly. If there is nothing to see, about the only way to obtain this essential information is to get it from the ship herself, by this method:

While in the straight reach, run parallel with and also close enough to the side on which the point will be (in this case the starboard side) so as to cause the ship "to be afraid of the bank" and therefore want to run away from it. This will cause her to carry considerable rudder. As soon as she begins to require less rudder to keep steady, it is an indication that the bend has been reached. At this moment, alter the course to the right sufficiently to bring the ship in toward the point. Soon she will require an increased amount of rudder. Keep her on this new heading until she once more begins to lose suction (or, in other words, carries less rudder), at which time again alter the course to the right. Continue this procedure until the ship is heading East.

It has just been implied that the foregoing procedure would

be necessary only during fog, darkness or some similar handicap, but now, because of the war, range and buoy lights are apt to be extinguished, and even day marks might be removed. Consequently, under present conditions this method of navigation might have to be resorted to in clear weather and even in the daytime. Furthermore, if enemy waters had to be entered, this might prove to be the most reliable guide.

When conditions are normal, and full speed or at least considerable headway can be maintained, it is almost always preferable to "keep in the bend" when making a turn. Therefore, the following explanation will be made as to why in times of poor visibility it is generally advisable to take the opposite side of the channel, or "cut the point" as it is called. It is for this reason: Only when working around the *point*—in making a turn—is it safe to let the ship's actions impart information for the sake of assistance. To elaborate on this statement: When the turn is reached and all during the time the turn is being made, the ship is heading toward deep water. So even in a narrow channel such a procedure makes possible a considerable delay in altering the course without getting into difficulty, because the ship can go diagonally across the channel before running aground. Hence the ship is in such a position that she can be navigated much more safely than the narrow channel and poor visibility would imply; and if she is a dependable ship, she can be relied upon "to smell her way around" the point.

Now contrast this with what would be the case if the ship were following the opposite bank (*i.e.*, the side the bend is on) when approaching the turn. Since she would already be carrying rudder it would be difficult, if not impossible, to detect just when she would signify—by carrying a little additional rudder—that the bend had been reached. The least bit of tardiness in altering the course would probably cause the ship to run aground; in fact, she might take the bank with her bow before there was any increase in suction abreast of the quarter. Furthermore, the ship's position would be precarious all during the time she was making the turn because it would be similar to heading into a cove.

3. KEEPING IN THE BEND

The preceding sections have shown how suction can be helpful in times of poor visibility, or when navigation aids are lacking. It is equally helpful in numerous other instances. But since it is so often disregarded, it might be well to explain how this happens and also to point out how the practice of ignoring its effects creates a grave potential danger that can suddenly and unexpectedly become a reality. Therefore, this chapter will accomplish its purpose if it does no more than cause the reader to become "suction conscious."

For the purpose of showing how suction is not only disregarded but furthermore how the person in charge may be—and often is—unaware of the effect it is having on the ship, the hypothetical channel described in the foregoing sections will again be used. Now, take it for granted conditions are such that the location of the channel is definitely known and that the ship can be run full speed. It was pointed out that the proper way to make the turn under these circumstances was "to keep in the bend" and thereby let suction help cause the desired swing.

However, the natural thing is to commence swinging too soon, or in other words "cut the point." If this is done, then the necessary swing can be accomplished only if the adverse effect of suction is not too great to be overcome by rudder power. To be specific: Suppose the man in charge of a ship is unaware of the effect that suction will have. When making a gradual bend in a narrow channel, he will almost invariably do the natural thing, which is to begin swinging a little too soon, with the result that the ship will feel the effect of the suction from the point. This will cause her to require, besides the amount of rudder normally necessary to make such a swing, whatever additional amount is necessary to counteract the retarding effect of the suction from the point.

For the sake of illustration suppose, if the suction could be neutralized or done away with, it would require 20 degrees of rudder to cause the necessary swing. Now suppose it takes 10 degrees of rudder to offset the retarding effect of the suction from the point. This would mean that 30 degrees of rudder would be required to make the turn. If he is not "suction conscious," the one in charge is almost certain to have a feeling of satisfaction that, by swinging a little early, he is taking a little extra precaution. But the ironical fact is this: The more cautious he intends to be, the more danger he is putting his ship in because, when making the turn in this manner, to have a little stronger head tide or a little heavier head wind might cause the ship to fail to answer, even with full rudder.

Criticism of this comment, very naturally, might be that the ship should be slowed down beforehand so as to be able to give her full speed when ready to make the turn and thereby do it more safely.

It will be readily agreed that this is a proper precaution whenever it is expected much rudder will be needed to make a turn; but note how this swing can be made with very little rudder. Before coming to the turn, the ship will be worked close enough up to the bend side of the channel so as to require about 10 degrees of rudder to hold her parallel with the bank, or in other words, to keep her from running away from it. When reaching the turn and in making it, she will be kept this distance out of the bend and will thereby get the benefit of an amount of suction that will cause as much of a swing as 10 degrees of rudder would. So to make the turn (recalling that with suction neutralized it would take 20 degrees), only 10 degrees of rudder will be required instead of 30 degrees; and by keeping still closer to the bank she might not need any assistance at all from the rudder.

4. MEETING AND PASSING ANOTHER VESSEL

The illustration cited in Section 3 requires something to counteract it emphatically, because not only do the proper way to make a bend and the proper way to pass a ship in a narrow channel seem like reckless indifference to those unfamiliar with close

Figure 1. This ship got too close to her starboard bank as she was about to pass another. Result: she is taking a sheer across the canal.

work but, very unfortunately indeed, after one does become accustomed to keeping close to the bank, or passing close to another vessel, then the reaction almost invariably is to go to the other extreme and want to keep too deep in a bend or to crowd a passing vessel too closely.

Both extremes of this impression are exemplified in a yarn about the Port Arthur Canal during the days when it was very narrow. A foreign ship was coming up the canal. Her captain—as she was about to meet another ship—suggested to the pilot that he give way; however, the pilot continued straight up the middle of the canal. After a bit the captain—a little more insistently—again suggested that he give way, but the pilot still continued straight ahead. A little later both ships gave way and as they passed without mishap the captain made this remark, "Ah! Now I understand. If you want to miss him, try to hit him."

Figure 2. Ship shown in Figure 1 has become "jacked."

Summarizing this chapter briefly: When about to meet another ship in a narrow channel, do not get over too far, or if the channel is very narrow, do not give way too soon; but it is also essential to guard against the mistake of not giving way enough at the proper time. These comments would be incomplete if the other important precaution were not, at least mentioned: Reduce headway.

5. Effect of Suction from Passing Ship

In a very general way, ships' meeting and keeping clear of one another has been taken care of. Fortunately, this can usually be done without trouble. However, in a narrow channel, after having passed another vessel, the ship is quite likely to take a sheer and strike the opposite bank. (This is especially apt to happen in a canal, because the suction is greater. For this reason, in the rest of the chapter, the channel may be assumed to be a canal unless otherwise stated.) Very special handling can, in numerous instances, prevent this mishap, so an explanation will be made of how prevention can best be accomplished. It might be helpful though to make some annotations first.

So far attention has been paid only to the effect on a ship of the suction she herself creates. But now, in conjunction therewith, the result of one ship's suction upon another ship will be considered. Suction is caused by two different things. One is the ship's headway, or—which amounts to the same thing—the action of the water passing by the ship in case she is anchored, moored or aground. The opinion seems to be quite prevalent that this is the only source, or at least that the other produces inconsequential effects. However, the other source, the suction caused by the propeller, is extremely important. For example, if the ship is dead in the water and the propeller is motionless, then there is no suction. But if the ship is aground or if for any other reason she cannot gather way, there will still be suction if the propeller turns; in fact with the propeller only turning over slowly, there is enough suction to cause its effects to be felt very decidedly when abreast of the quarter and close to it; of course, the faster the propeller turns the stronger is the suction and the farther out it is felt. It might be well to elaborate on this by saying that the wheel water which is plainly visible directly astern of the ship (when the propeller is working ahead), is only vaguely thought and spoken of as suction. It is abreast the quarter, where the water apparently has the least motion and apparently is the least harmful, that, in reality, it is the most powerful and dangerous.

Mention must also be made of a thing that always exists when a ship has way on her, and is most always thought of either as suction, or in connection with suction. It is a ship's bow wave. Its effects are negligible or slight when the ship is going slow, but can be very pronounced in confined waters—especially from a loaded ship making much headway.

With these remarks as a guide, the problem to consider is how best to avoid losing control of the ship just after passing another

—by making proper allowances for the ship's own created suction, and in addition, making appropriate allowance for the effect of another ship's suction.

Assume the canal is of such width that, with each ship giving way the maximum amount possible without getting too close to the bank, there will then be, roughly, 50 feet or more of space between them when they are abreast of one another. We will have them pass in the conventional manner, *i.e.*, port to port.

The explanation must revert to where the ships were approaching one another. (Both ships should follow the actions described, but the actual handling of only one will be considered.) In ample time the ship should be slowed down as much as is possible without sacrificing good control over her. Presume conditions are such that with the engine working slow ahead she handles satisfactorily.

In approaching the other ship she is kept far enough away from her starboard bank to make certain the suction from the bank will not prevent her from readily answering her right rudder at the necessary time.

Now just a little before the bows get close, both ships give considerable right rudder with the result that each heads decidedly toward her own starboard bank; and then shortly afterward each reverses the rudder so as to throw their respective sterns clear; then each steadies up. At the completion of this combination of maneuvers the position of each ship is parallel with and *close to* her starboard bank. (From now on the other ship's maneuvers will not be noted.)

When the ship under consideration gets parallel with the bank —because of the fact that she is so close alongside of it—she will require a great deal of right rudder (probably in the neighborhood of 20 degrees) to keep steady. Her proximity to the bank might be such that full right rudder would be insufficient except for the effect of the bow wave—between her bow and the other ship's side—which is a decided help in keeping her from going to port. Shortly after being steadied up, her bow will be abreast the quarter of the other ship. When this position is reached, the suction coming from the other ship's quarter will suddenly pull the bow to port. (This is true of both ships, but only the one whose movements are being observed will be considered.) It would seem to be the logical thing to give more right rudder. That is what will (for the sake of illustration) be done, and by putting it full right the swing is stopped. But the bow quickly gets beyond this influence (*i.e.,* the suction from the other ship's quarter) so the wheel is eased up and by the time it is about amidships the stern has gotten to where it is feeling this pull—which is much stronger than the suction from the bank—so she heads in still closer.

However, the other ship's suction is soon lost. And when it is our ship is so close to the bank that the combined effect of full right rudder and full speed ahead is insufficient to overcome the bank's suction. Much to the dismay of the man in charge, our ship goes across the canal and strikes the opposite side.

Naturally the question arises: Could this mishap have been prevented? The subsequent illustration will serve as an answer. But first, attention should be called to a special condition that helped, slightly, to cause the mishap: When a ship has headway and the engine is working ahead, the zone of effect created by the wheel water and the other disturbances directly astern—especially when a shoal, or some such condition, retards the speed— makes a pattern somewhat similar to the upper part of a fleur-de-lis. Which is to say, an object directly astern will be forced farther astern, but an object on either side of astern will be forced farther off to the side.

Therefore, immediately after the passing, our ship came under an influence that forced her stern toward the bank, thereby aggravating the already unfavorable condition.

A ship, immediately after passing another ship, will go contrary to full rudder although at any other time she might answer her rudder in spite of being equally close to the bank. It takes more rudder to counteract bank suction immediately after passing another ship than at any other time.

Getting back to the illustration, we will proceed with our ship just the same as in the foregoing account up to the time the ships were abreast of one another. Then, although the bow does take a rank sheer toward the other ship's quarter (and here begins the knack of keeping control) it will be allowed to go quite a bit in that direction, because there is very little likelihood of its striking the other ship's quarter since the other ship's stern is moving out of the way. So we let our ship's head swing out to about the middle of the canal. Shortly after the bow heads out, the stern of our ship will get the effect of the suction from the other ship's quarter. When this happens (and here is the remainder of the knack), let the other ship's suction pull our ship's stern away from the bank. Also at this time she should be given full speed, for two reasons. First, so as to overcome more surely the lateral effect of the other ship's wheel water, or wake; second, she will be near enough to the middle of the canal so as to make it quite certain that rudder power will predominate over bank suction. (This will be more fully covered in Section 9, Chapter I.)

If the canal is so narrow that there is very limited space between the ships when they are abreast, then there *is* serious danger of each ship's bow being sucked into the other ship's quarter. In such cases this method of passing must not be resorted to.[2]

6. Contour of Bank Governs Strength of Suction

With regard to bank suction there is another fact that deserves comment: Whenever the bank is perfectly straight up and down—like the wall of a lock—the suction is less than when the bank is sloping. Going a step farther with the explanation: With one

[2] How ships might more safely pass in a very narrow canal or channel will be found in Situation 3, Chapter VI.

bank of a canal vertical and the other one sloping, to keep a ship in the middle she will carry rudder toward the sloping bank, *i.e.,* she will want to run away from the sloping bank.

7. PASSING A MOORED VESSEL

In the beginning it was stated that the increased speed and size of ships have made it important to take more precaution in regard to the effect of suction. When a vessel is moored in a narrow channel she will feel the disturbance in the water that is caused by a ship going full speed while the ship under way is still several miles off. (This does not refer to the heavy bow wave directly ahead of the ship.) Therefore, before approaching any closer than this to the moored vessel, the ship should be slowed down. If the way is reduced so that she is making only dead slow speed, then the disturbance (or it seems appropriate to call it ground swell) that goes ahead is not appreciably felt more than about a quarter of a mile; in fact at this speed she is going slow enough so as not to cause too great an effect when passing. However, at this distance the propeller should be stopped because its motion will begin to be felt slightly (when a quarter of a mile away) and will continue to be felt increasingly till directly abreast the moored vessel, at which time—although working only dead slow—the propeller will cause the moored vessel to surge heavily on her lines. Briefly, to pass a moored vessel safely, reduce headway soon enough to allow the disturbance that goes ahead of a ship to subside; then stop the propeller shortly before getting abreast of the moored vessel and headreach by.

8. FLOATING A GROUNDED VESSEL

A ship's headway causes annoyance to moored vessels but, conversely, it is a boon to vessels that are aground. For example, if a ship goes full speed—or even just with considerable headway—

close by a vessel that is on the bottom, she will often cause the grounded vessel to get afloat, in spite of the fact that various other attempts to free her might have failed.

Whenever resorting to this method there is a precaution that should be taken. The vessel that is aground should keep her propeller motionless while the ship under way is approaching and until she is sufficiently past.

A person cannot "lift himself by his bootstraps"; however, a ship is capable of doing a thing that is, seemingly, as impossible. She can sometimes use her own swell to lift herself over a shoal. Suppose a ship is going full speed in a narrow channel and suddenly fetches up on a lump, causing her to come to a complete stop. Just a trifle later the swell, that has been following astern, will overtake her and frequently has lifting power enough to cause the ship to get afloat—with the assistance of full speed ahead on the engine.

9. Getting Away from a Bank: Rudder Power Versus Suction

"Having a bear by the tail and not knowing how to turn him loose" is just about the same predicament that a ship may be in when she gets too close to a bank and does not know how to let go of the suction, because she is under two conflicting influences, suction and rudder power. If suction predominates, she "goes wild." To illustrate, suppose a "bad" ship (in this case it would mean one that is weak on rudder power and is also strongly affected by suction) is close to and parallel with the starboard bank and is dead in the water. It is desired to get her in the center of the canal. The engine is worked dead slow ahead; the rudder is left amidships because, although she must not run away from the bank too quickly, it is also important that she should immediately start swinging out a little.

Since she is a "bad" ship her stern begins gradually drawing toward the bank as soon as the propeller starts turning. The rudder is put over until it is full right; but still her head goes to port. When she has swung out 3 or 4 degrees the engine's speed is then increased to slow—with the rudder, of course, kept full right. This momentarily causes her to steady up, but soon afterward she again starts swinging gradually to port. When she has headed out about 6 or 7 degrees she is given half speed ahead.

Figure 3. Ship was encountering a strong head tide. She got too close to her port bank and, in sheering away from it, the current helped to force her against the starboard bank so hard she became grounded. Strength of current can be detected by noting how the tugs are lying nearly broadside to it while pulling on the ship.

This again causes her to steady up for a while, but a little later the suction again predominates, and she once more goes against her rudder. When she is headed out about 10 degrees, or when her bow is nearly in the middle (the wider the canal the farther she can, and should, be allowed to swing), she is given full speed. The one in command heaves a sigh of relief! She not only steadies up but also begins answering her right rudder, because her quarter has gotten far enough away from the bank to enable the wheel water on the rudder to predominate.

To go into more detail about this illustration: With the stern staying in the same position, the suction created by the wheel water is at its minimum (with regard to any particular number of revolutions of the propeller) the instant speed is increased; therefore, the rudder will predominate over suction immediately after speed is increased more than at any later time.

It has just been pointed out that when a ship is lying alongside of a canal bank, dead in the water, it is difficult to keep control while maneuvering her into the middle. So naturally, getting close when she has headway makes it still more probable that she will "go wild"; and if she should get very close while going full speed, then it is almost a hopeless case because there is no further resort left. (See Figure 3.) Therefore, when circumstances make such an eventuality probable, it is prudent to set the speed at half —or preferably slow, or dead slow—so as to be able to break a sheer with full speed.

10. Passing Open Water: Suction Versus Bow Wave

The undesirable (or harmful) and the desirable (or helpful) influences that sometimes affect a ship can be so nearly evenly matched—or pitted against one another—that, on occasions, keeping control over a ship depends mainly upon making helpful influences outweigh or overcome harmful ones. "Rudder power versus suction" has just been analyzed.

Now "suction versus bow wave" will be considered. Misinterpretation of the previous comments (in Section 5, Chapter I) about the bow wave probably would give it undue credit, because when a ship is going anywhere near head-on—even toward a substantial object such as a loaded ship, a bank or a quay—the bow wave's ability to "fend-off" a ship is negligible. Its action is of significance, on the ship herself, only when the relation is to something to which she is running practically parallel. In such cases it acts—very decidedly, and especially on a loaded ship— as a wedge in deflecting the bow.

To illustrate suction versus bow wave, here is an instance taken from the history of a canal in which, at one time, there was a set of locks. Later, it was decided to discontinue the use of these locks; but it was simpler to dig a by-pass than to remove them. The by-pass and the canal resembled a siding, and a straight stretch of railway track. Inbound the by-pass was on the starboard side.

After all but the upper extremity of the by-pass had been dug, numerous inbound loaded ships had this experience: They could be kept steady in the center of the canal until they got to the by-pass. Then they would go into the by-pass in spite of full left rudder. The reason: When the forward part of the ship got to the by-pass the pressure of the bow wave on the starboard bow was practically eliminated. With the suction the same on both quarters, the pressure of the bow wave on the port bow predominated. This problem was overcome by pitting suction against bow wave in the following manner:

The canal was so narrow a ship had to be kept practically in the center to prevent her from "going wild." Therefore, she would be held in the middle until shortly before she got to the by-pass. Then the starboard bank would be favored enough to cause the suction from it (on the ship's starboard quarter) to make the ship want to sheer to port just at the time she would otherwise be wanting to sheer to starboard.

Another explanation for the ship wanting to go into the by-pass—recalling that in this book vessels are being personified—is this: Not only are ships afraid of shoal water, but it is equally true that "instinct" tells them to "take the course of least resistance," which in this case was to go into the by-pass.

11. MAKING A SHARP BEND: SUCTION COORDINATED WITH BOW WAVE

Suction *versus* bow wave has been commented on. Now suction *in coordination with* bow wave will be considered.

It is a universally recognized fact that when the rudder is put over and thereby causes a ship's head to go in one direction, then the ship will go broadside or "skid" or "crab" toward the opposite side.

When a ship is making a sharp bend in a channel this skidding, or sidewise motion, is less than it would be if the ship were in open water because the bank acts as a wall in fending her off.

To what extent it acts in this manner depends upon the effectiveness of the bow wave, in conjunction with the pressure of the water between the ship's side and the bank; and this in turn depends principally on the draft of the ship and the contour of the bank in the bend.

On a light ship the bow wave's fending-off effect will be: (1) almost negligible, if in the bend there is a flat with a considerable amount of water on it, because this condition is almost the same as if the ship were in open water; (2) slightly effective if the bank is practically vertical from the bed of the channel to the surface of the water.

On a loaded ship—and especially if her draft puts her down to where she is just clear of the bed of the channel—the fending-off action will (1) be somewhat effective, if in the bend there is a flat with a considerable amount of water on it; (2) almost entirely eliminate the sidewise motion, if the bank is nearly vertical.

Thus, when suction helps the rudder to pull the stern in, the bow wave, in conjunction with the pressure of the water between the bank and the ship's side, exerts an opposite influence varying in degree from slightly modifying to almost entirely eliminating the undesirable sidewise or skidding motion.

12. Determining Direction of Current

So far the effect of current has been ignored, but when under way in a canal, and especially at night, it is very desirable and sometimes extremely important to know in which direction the current is running, or if it is slack.

In some inland waterways—and especially in those bordering the coast of the Gulf of Mexico—the direction of the current is subject to sudden change and is generally unpredictable. Furthermore, at times, it runs with considerable strength.

If no other means of finding out is available, the direction of the current can be judged surprisingly well by noticing how the ship acts at the turns. If she sets toward the point it is an indication of a head tide; whereas if she sets toward the bend, it is an indication of a fair tide. (See Figure 4.)

It would probably be impossible to tell exactly—on paper— just when to start a ship to swinging, when making a bend; however, the following comments should be helpful.

With a strong head tide, the swinging should be delayed the longest; with a slack tide, begin swinging a little sooner; and when there is a strong fair tide, the swinging should be commenced the earliest.

13. Effects of Head Tide and Fair Tide

To go into further detail about the difference in the effect of a head tide and that of a fair tide: From the safety standpoint the head tide is preferable because a ship can easily be stopped, if necessary; and if she takes a rank enough sheer to cause her bow to become grounded, she will not get "jacked."

However, a ship will steer much better with a fair tide. This fact can probably be best exemplified by considering an extreme case: A very bad steering ship in a narrow canal where there is a two-knot current.

In connection with the illustration these two facts will be pointed out: (1) The less the headway, the less the ship's steering will be affected by bank and bottom suction. (2) In a confined channel a vessel, under way, does not always float freely. For example, when close alongside of a bank and making headway, a vessel might have her bow forced out and at the same time have her stern drawn in.

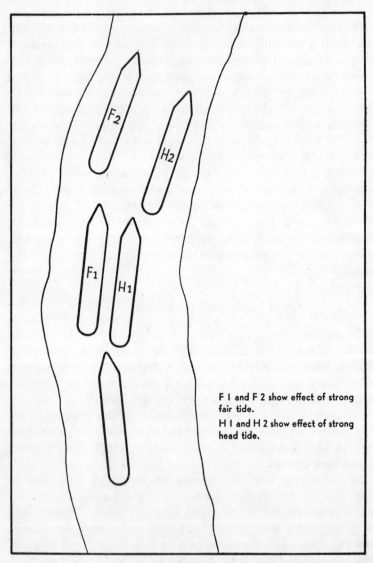

F 1 and F 2 show effect of strong fair tide.

H 1 and H 2 show effect of strong head tide.

Figure 4

22

When making two knots through the water and encountering a two-knot head tide, a ship would be merely holding her own. Since ill effect of suction increases proportionately as speed increases (so that with greater speed an uncontrollable sheer is more apt to develop), if the vessel went fast enough through the water to advance appreciably over the bottom, she might be making too much headway to be kept under control.

On the other hand, with a two-knot fair tide, a bad steering ship making two knots through the water in a narrow canal could get over the bottom quite satisfactorily.

To summarize: A very "bad" ship can be kept under control and will get over the bottom with a strong fair tide because she needs to make very little, if any, headway. Whereas with the same strength of head tide, the speed she will have to make to get over the bottom will cause her to go wild. This is accounted for, primarily, by the fact that the more the speed, the more the suction.

But there is still another reason why the head tide causes a ship to fail to answer her rudder as well as she does with a fair tide.

With a head tide, whenever a ship gets close enough to either side to cause the suction to draw the quarter toward the bank, at the same time the tide together with the congestion of water beween the ship's side and the bank begins striking most heavily on the ship's inshore side. This volume of water takes the shape of a wedge and consequently forces her bow out, *i.e.*, causes her to want to sheer. As the speed increases, the "wedge" of water, between the ship's side and the bank, becomes more powerful. (These facts are more fully explained in Section 1, Chapter II, and Figure 7.)

But with a strong fair tide, since the ship needs to have only slight headway through the water to enable her to advance satisfactorily over the bottom, the ill effect of the "wedge" and of suction is at a minimum.

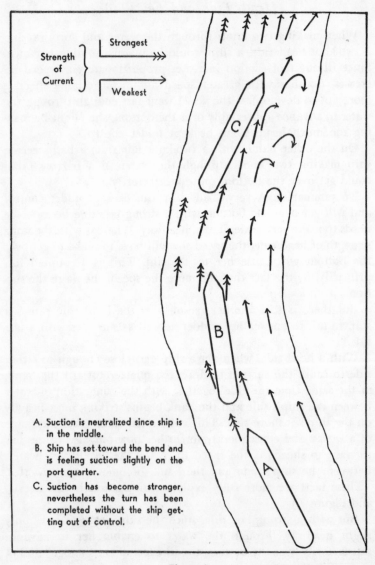

Strength of Current
Strongest ⟫⟫⟫
Weakest →

C

B

A

A. Suction is neutralized since ship is in the middle.

B. Ship has set toward the bend and is feeling suction slightly on the port quarter.

C. Suction has become stronger, nevertheless the turn has been completed without the ship getting out of control.

Figure 5

To make the explanation clearer, suppose the ship to be heading with the current, but to be dead in the water. She would be going over the bottom at the rate of two knots per hour. However, even though she might be close to the bank, there nevertheless would be no "wedge" or congestion of water to cause her to want to sheer.

Whereas, if the ship were heading against the current, she could be making a speed of two knots through the water and yet she would be stationary over the bottom. In this case, if she were close enough to the bank to cause her stern to be drawn in by suction, then a "wedge" or congestion of water would be formed which would cause the ship to want to sheer.

14. MAKING A SHARP BEND WITH A STRONG FAIR TIDE

If the ship, especially if she is loaded, is in a certain position when under way with a strong fair tide, the pattern the current makes at the bends may have a pronounced tendency to cause her to want to swing too much. As a rule, the current runs most strongly on the bend side of the channel; whereas "under the point" there is apt to be an eddy. Therefore, in making a sharp turn, if the full force of the current strikes the ship on the quarter and at the same time her bow is in water that is slack or running in the opposite direction, then, as the saying goes, "She will want to turn around and look at herself." Now if to these two current conditions is added the influence of excessive suction, there is serious danger of the ship turning completely around, or going crosswise, if the channel is too narrow to turn in.

To avoid this predicament the bend should be approached in a manner that will minimize and, most nearly neutralize, suction as well as avoid getting in these contra-currents. (See Figure 5.)

Suction is minimized by proceeding slowly through the water. It is entirely neutralized as long as it is felt as strongly on one quarter as it is on the other; generally speaking, this condition exists when in the middle of the channel.

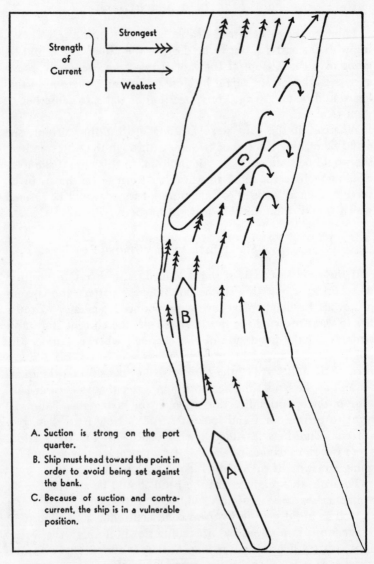

Strength of Current

Strongest
>>>

Weakest
>

A. Suction is strong on the port quarter.
B. Ship must head toward the point in order to avoid being set against the bank.
C. Because of suction and contra-current, the ship is in a vulnerable position.

Figure 6

So instead of "keeping in the bend" as is most generally advisable, and sometimes necessary, the ship should be about in the middle of the channel and going at slow speed when approaching the turn.

Although starting the swing from this position, the ship will set quite a bit toward the bend side of the channel before the turn is completed. (See Section 12, Chapter I and Figure 4.)

As soon as she gets a little nearer to the bend side of the channel she will commence getting suction to help her to swing, and in addition to this (since she will be set toward the bend), she will have to be headed, at least slightly, diagonal to the direction of the channel. This position will cause the current, also, to help in the swinging.

On the other hand, for the sake of picturing a ship in a vulnerable position, suppose she approaches the turn from near the bend side of the channel. (See Figure 6.)

When arriving at the turn, she will have to head decidedly toward the opposite (or point) side of the channel to avoid having the current set her against the bank.

This diagonal heading will cause the after part of the ship to be struck by fair current where it is running most strongly, forcing the ship to swing. Bank suction will aggravate this swing still more. Then, in addition to these two influences, the bow will be in, or at least close to, slack water, or current that is running in the opposite direction.

While the ship was approaching this position (shown in Figure 6, position C), something else has been taking place: When a deep-loaded ship is swinging heavily (as she would have to do after arriving at position B in Figure 6—or else be set into the bend), it requires full rudder against the swing for some considerable length of time in order to break, or stop the swing, even though the ship is entirely free from suction, current or any other extraneous influence. Therefore this swing adds, still more, to the ship's vulnerability.

15. Passing a Tow

It often happens that a ship comes upon and desires to pass a slower craft of some kind or, more probably, a tow. Instead of telling how it should be done, an account will be given of what is apt to occur when the passing is done; first, with considerable —but not necessarily excessive—headway.

Suppose a loaded ship with her engine working full, but making somewhat less than full speed because of being in a shallow and narrow canal, is overtaking a tug on a short bridle ahead of a loaded scow barge.[3] Assume the overall length of the tow is not more than 250 feet. If the tug continues pulling full speed then the ship, from necessity, will have to work her engine about half speed in order to continue overtaking. Assume that, while the ship is still some distance astern, the tow hauls over to one side so as to give sufficient passing room, but continues pulling full speed. The ship, holding about the center of the canal (because getting over appreciably would cause her to get too much bank suction), continues overtaking the tow until just before the bow of the ship has come up to a position slightly astern of abreast of the stern of the barge. When arriving at this position the ship's bow wave will begin to act on the barge about the same as a comber acts on a surf board when it is being ridden. The bow wave might be so high that it would lift the barge's stern enough so that the barge would "run before it"; but presume the wave is not that high and consequently the tow drops back.

This comment about the bow wave might seem erroneous because in open water its shape conforms, roughly, to the ship's bow; but in a narrow canal it makes a swell about at right angles to the ship's heading because the bank is so close.

In addition to this swell there still remains—close around the

[3] In the principal canals, most tugs have three or four barges in tow. A single barge is used in the illustration for the sake of making the explanation clearer.

bow—the repelling action of the water. Consequently when the barge is broad on the ship's bow the effect of the wave will shove, or breast, the barge away from the ship and thereby cause it to sheer some, but not too much for the tug to control.

When the tug gets astern of the bow wave, the tow will then drop back without abnormal influence until the stern of the barge gets abreast the ship's quarter. Then the barge will get a swell that runs approximately at right angles to the ship's heading. This swell will act on the barge in the same manner as the bow wave, only much more strongly. Therefore, even though the barge readily dropped astern of the bow wave, she might on the other hand—with the ship going at the same speed—continue to run before, or stay ahead of, the stern swell. For the sake of illustration, assume that the barge does stay ahead of this swell. In this case the barge will immediately take up the speed of the ship—irrespective of the tug's pulling. Now suppose the ship increases speed for the purpose of causing the barge to drop astern. The outcome will be exactly opposite to that which is desired, because increasing the speed will simply make the ship's stern swell higher and stronger, and thereby make it more impossible for the barge to drop back.

It would be fortunate indeed if this were the only effect the action of the ship's water had on the tow. But this much headway is almost certain to cause something much more serious. When the stern of the barge gets this swell she also gets the ship's suction which will pull the after part of the barge in alongside the ship's quarter. This in turn will cause the barge's bow to sheer away from the ship. When this happens, if the tug has engine power and rudder power enough to break the sheer, she will be able to pull the barge's bow in toward the ship. With suction—at the same time—pulling the stern in, the barge will almost invariably land broadside against the ship so easily she "wouldn't break an egg shell."

But on the other hand, when the suction causes the sheer, suppose the tug does not have the power to break it. Then the bow of the barge will go away from the ship and cause the tug to trip or to let go. While this is happening, the after part of the barge will be sucked up under the quarter; how far, and whether or not she strikes the rudder and propeller depends almost solely on the respective drafts of the barge and the ship. After having gotten in this position the barge, in all probability, will drop astern—because she will have gotten behind the swell.

These facts stated briefly are: (a) The action of the water around a ship's bow can be very heavy, but it is not likely to cause much trouble because its characteristic is to shove an object away; (b) from abaft the forecastlehead to forward of the poop deck is a safe area because the water is normal, or in other words runs parallel with the side of the ship; (c) the water abreast the ship's quarter is the most dangerous, first, because there it is the most powerful; and, second, because it does what suction implies —it draws an object in; and furthermore, the closer in an object gets, the stronger the suction gets.

It might seem as though the action of the water abreast the overtaking ship's quarter, or in its vicinity, did not always have a drawing-in effect but, at times, had a repelling effect. Occasionally, when the overtaken craft has dropped back till her stern is abreast of the ship's quarter, instead of having her stern drawn in, she experiences what might seem to be the opposite; *i.e.*, her *bow* will take an uncontrollable sheer *toward* the ship's side. (This may happen especially if there is sufficient space so that she does not get too strong a pull from the overtaking ship's quarter.)

This might make it appear that the sheer was caused by the stern of the craft being forced out. However, this is the explanation of what takes place:

To begin with, instead of the overtaking of a tow, consider the overtaking of a self-propelled vessel about 200 feet long.

This vessel will be likened to a column with one end resting on the ground. The column can sway slightly and still stand. But let it tilt too much and then gravity will cause it to fall.

The stern of the vessel resembles the lower end of the column; and the swell—running at right angles to the ship's heading—resembles the ground. From about abaft the forecastlehead to abreast the poop deck, the water—running aft and parallel with the ship's side—has an effect on the vessel similar to the effect that gravity has on the column. The vessel may sheer slightly and recover; but let her sheer too much—either in or out—and then the sheer cannot be controlled.

Now it will be assumed the same ship is overtaking the same tow with all related facts the same, except that this time the tow slows down before the ship comes upon it. Consequently the ship reduces speed to dead slow and still continues overtaking. The bow wave is trivial so it has no noticeable effects on the tow; the ship continues passing till the suction from her quarter catches the barge's stern, and thereby causes her to sheer slightly. The tug "hooks up" (goes full speed) for a few moments and easily breaks the sheer, and then again slows down; as the ship has only a slight stern swell, the tow quickly drops back without incident.

If it should be necessary that the ship create the least possible disturbance in passing, it can best be accomplished in this manner: The tow should get practically dead in the water before being overtaken; and the ship should approach at dead slow speed. When the tow gets in the "safe area," *i.e.*, between the forecastlehead and the poop, the ship should stop her engine. This will entirely eliminate the only source of suction which is of any consequence in this case, namely: the suction from the propeller. Although the ship's headway is only slight, she will easily carry her headway long enough—being loaded—to get by, provided the tug pulls only strongly enough to keep herself and her tow under control.

16. Using Suction to Advantage

In summarizing these comments it can be said: Suction is generally thought of only as a handicap, or as a source of trouble; but by taking proper precautions, its harmful effects can be satisfactorily offset. Furthermore, suction can (1) give invaluable information, on occasion, when navigating a narrow channel; (2) help in making a bend; (3) frequently, by utilizing a passing vessel's suction, prevent a ship from getting out of control, after the passing is completed; (4) often be a most effective means of getting a vessel afloat; (5) in various situations, be made to act as an auxiliary to the rudder.

In taking advantage of these facts one is MAKING SUCTION AN ASSET.

Chapter Two

Anchoring

1. ANCHORING AGAINST A VERTICAL BANK

When the banks of a channel, or waterway, are soft mud and when they are nearly straight up and down it is possible for an anchored ship to lie against them—provided it is properly done—with little, if any, more likelihood of her getting into difficulties, or of sustaining damage, than when lying alongside of a dock. Fortunately this is true, because in some inland waters this is a necessary practice.

When such waterways are narrow, ships must be anchored so as not to obstruct navigation; and where there is both an ebb and flood tide, special precaution should be taken in order to have swinging room as well as to safeguard against "jacking" (lying stern to the tide on the anchor) when the tide turns.

Suppose a channel having the above characteristics is about 600 feet wide and a ship[1] must be put to anchor where she can lie for an indefinite period of time.

If she were anchored in the middle of the channel she very probably would be too much of an obstruction to navigation; and when the tide turned she would not have sufficient room to swing. Even though the current ran downstream continuously, there would still be the likelihood of the ship's stern getting against the bank in case of a strong beam wind. Therefore, if it would be

[1] See footnote, page 3.

extremely difficult, or impossible, to keep the ship clear of the bank, the safest and most desirable place to anchor is: (1) close to either side where the bank is nearly vertical, so as to avoid grounding (and also for another reason that will be commented on later); (2) where the channel runs straight, or nearly straight, for at least three ship lengths so as to have a straight reach to lie in with either tide; (3) where the channel runs straight because it is more probable then that the current will run straight; and by avoiding "crooked water" one cause of the ship's not wanting to lie to her anchor is eliminated.

Under favorable conditions a ship will lie satisfactorily on one anchor, with a short scope of chain, when it is dropped close alongside of the bank; and when she does, that will be sufficient. Then too it might be that the channel is straight and the shore line is unobstructed for a considerable distance so that ample chain to safeguard against dragging can be given on a single anchor.

However, at times a ship will not lie on one anchor. Some of the possible, if not probable, difficulties that can come about by using only one anchor will be pointed out. They are materially lessened, and often entirely eliminated, by the proper use of two anchors.

In all of the illustrations it will be taken for granted the ship will be anchored where the channel is straight and that the bank is near enough vertical to eliminate the possibility of the ship's getting on top of the bank while she is lying parallel to it.

First assume the tide is running very strong and that there is unlimited clearance both ahead and astern so that there is no need to be concerned about the distance the ship takes up along the shore line; consequently—with a feeling of security—only one anchor is dropped and given, say, 60 fathoms of chain. However, in all probability the ship will get into difficulties.

Before pointing out these potential complications, though, an explanation will be made as to why a ship is apt not to want to

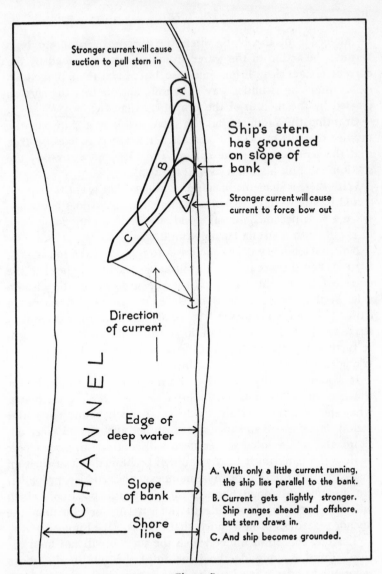

Stronger current will cause suction to pull stern in

Ship's stern has grounded on slope of bank

Stronger current will cause current to force bow out

CHANNEL

Direction of current

Edge of deep water

Slope of bank

Shore line

A. With only a little current running, the ship lies parallel to the bank.

B. Current gets slightly stronger. Ship ranges ahead and offshore, but stern draws in.

C. And ship becomes grounded.

Figure 7

35

lie alongside of the bank when the current is running. It is because the action of the water around the stern, caused by the current, creates a condition similar to, but milder than, that which exists when she is under way. The difference is that the suction created by the motion of the propeller is lacking.

Granting the premise that the more headway a ship has, the heavier the suction will be abreast her stern; it is likewise true that the more strongly the current runs, the more strongly the suction will pull her stern toward the bank.

With these statements in mind, consider what is apt to happen —and for the sake of the illustration we will say does happen— when a ship lies anchored alongside the bank on one long scope of chain, with a strong current running.

Now the tendency of the suction is to pull the stern toward the bank. When this occurs the ship no longer is directly head to the current but, instead, has it a little the stronger on the inshore side. With nothing to hold the bow, it naturally sheers out a little. This in turn causes still more of the force of the current to strike on the inshore side; and, in addition, the current's strength is further intensified by its constriction within the wedge, or triangle, that is formed by the ship and the bank.

It would naturally seem that the next sequence would be for the current to force the ship broadside offshore. Nevertheless, what she is almost certain to do—except when one particular condition exists—is to range ahead on her anchor and sheer offshore. But while doing so her stern will continue to draw closer against the bank until finally she will be headed out at such an angle that her quarter, or to be more exact her rudder, propeller, etc., becomes grounded. She will then lie in this position—which will be practically broadside to the current—or else drag the anchor regardless of how much chain is out. (See Figure 7.)

The one condition under which the suction will not hold the ship's quarter alongside the bank until she gets in the above mentioned position is when the bank is practically vertical from

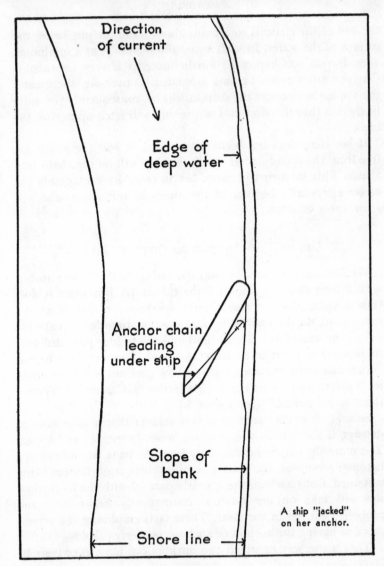

Direction
of current

Edge of
deep water

Anchor chain
leading
under ship

Slope of
bank

A ship "jacked"
on her anchor.

Shore line

Figure 8

37

the bed of the channel to a point above water, or just below the surface of the water. In such a case the suction is at a minimum. (See Section 6, Chapter I.) Furthermore, it is very improbable that the quarter can become grounded. Conversely, the greater the slope, the stronger the suction will be, consequently the more likely it is that the after part of the ship will fetch up against the bank.

If her stern does not become grounded, it will eventually get free from the suction, after which the ship will let the chain lead ahead. This in turn will cause her to come back alongside the bank; afterward—because of the aforesaid influences—she will again sheer offshore.

2. USE OF TWO ANCHORS TO PREVENT "JACKING"

We will next assume the ship lies satisfactorily on one anchor with a long scope of chain till the tide turns. But when it does turn suppose that for some reason, perhaps because of an on-shore wind, she does not swing with the tide. In order to make her swing, the engine is worked ahead and the rudder put hard over to throw her stern away from the bank. But contrary to our desires her stern draws in and her bow goes out until the chain leads astern and comes tight. (See Section 9, Chapter I.) Then— the ship is "jacked." (See Figure 8.)

Strange as it may seem it is very seldom that a ship sustains damage if she gets in this position; nevertheless, it can happen. The more the ship is headed away from the bank when her stern becomes grounded, the more possibility there is of damage being sustained. Conversely, if she is nearly parallel with the bank, then she will take on her quarter—consequently her rudder and propeller will be in the clear. These facts emphasize the importance of having the anchor, or anchors, properly placed.

This is the way in which two anchors can most effectively be

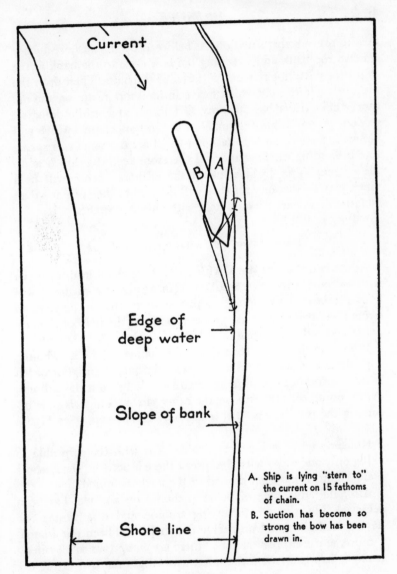

Current

Edge of
deep water

Slope of bank

Shore line

A. Ship is lying "stern to"
   the current on 15 fathoms
   of chain.
B. Suction has become so
   strong the bow has been
   drawn in.

Figure 9

used to prevent this situation. As before, drop the offshore anchor close to the bank and—keeping the bow close to the bank as the ship drops astern—pay out 60 fathoms of chain. Then drop the inshore anchor, after which heave in, or shorten up, on the offshore chain till it has out only 45 fathoms and, while doing so, pay out on the inshore chain. Now the inshore chain—which will be leading astern with 15 fathoms—will act the same as a spring line in holding the bow and will therefore keep the ship head to the current. The 45 fathoms on the offshore anchor will hold much better— because the ship will lie head to the current—than 60 fathoms, or more, would hold with only one anchor out.

3. Anchoring to Swing with the Tide

Now when the tide turns, with the inshore chain leading astern with so short a scope (15 fathoms), in acting as a spring it will keep the bow close enough inshore so as to enable the stern to swing away from the bank, probably without the help of the propeller and rudder, or with their help, if needed. (See Figure 9.)

When the ship gets crosswise of the channel as she is swinging with the tide, slack out on what was the inshore chain (but which is now becoming the offshore chain) till it has out 45 fathoms. While doing so, heave in on the other chain (which is now becoming the inshore one) till it has only 15 fathoms. (See Figure 10.)

Not only will "jacking" be avoided but with the ship able to swing only one way—with the spread there is between the anchors —the chains cannot get crossed or the anchors fouled.

Also, the advantage of being anchored on a swivel has been achieved, but the accompanying trouble and disadvantage of having to shackle and unshackle the chains has been eliminated.

Since, as the expression goes, "there are exceptions to all rules," it might happen—when the tide turns—that even by putting the

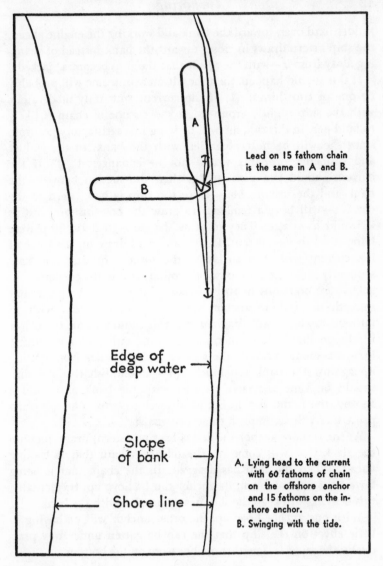

Lead on 15 fathom chain is the same in A and B.

Edge of deep water →

Slope of bank →

Shore line →

A. Lying head to the current with 60 fathoms of chain on the offshore anchor and 15 fathoms on the inshore anchor.

B. Swinging with the tide.

Figure 10

41

rudder hard over, toward the bank and working the engine ahead, the ship's stern draws in closer toward the bank instead of swinging away from it—with the result that the ship becomes "jacked."

If this should happen, then the ultimate outcome will probably be one of two things: (1) If the current runs only moderately, with the ship slightly grounded, a short scope of chain is likely to hold her. In this case she will be lying in a satisfactory position, since she will be nearly parallel with the bank, so the rudder and propeller probably would not be endangered. (2) If the current should run very strong, then the suction between the bank and the inshore *bow*—since the ship is lying stern to the current—will have a tendency to draw the bow inshore, just as it would have a tendency to draw the stern in if the ship were lying head to the current. If the bow does draw in, the force of the current will then strike on the inshore quarter and consequently cause the ship to swing around head to the current.

On rare occasions neither of these things will take place, but instead, the inshore anchor, which is leading astern with 15 fathoms of chain, will drag. In case this should occur, the officer in charge should have in mind avoiding either of two things: First, he should prevent the rudder and propeller from getting up against the bank too much. (To accomplish this the ship should be kept as nearly parallel with the bank as possible.) Second, the chains should not be allowed to cross. The following procedure will accomplish these two goals:

As the inshore anchor (which is leading astern) drags, pick up the slack that will come on the offshore chain that is leading ahead. When the ship has dragged till the chain that is being hove on is up and down, its anchor can be hove up. Incidentally, this heaving will keep the ship nearly parallel with the bank.

With one anchor hove up, the other anchor will be having so little effect on the ship that she can be gotten under way practically the same as if neither anchor were on the bottom.

4. ANCHORING ON A SHORT SCOPE OF CHAIN

Next assume only a moderate tide to be running, but that the clearance ahead and astern is limited and therefore it is necessary to anchor on the shortest possible scope of chain. To accomplish this, drop the offshore anchor as close to the bank as it can be gotten and a trifle ahead of the center of what will be the length of shore line the ship will require in swinging to both tides. Let the ship drop astern till 15 fathoms of chain has been paid out. Then, with the bow close to the bank, drop the inshore anchor and pay out on both chains till the offshore anchor has 30 fathoms and the inshore anchor has 15 fathoms.

When the tide slacks, shorten up the offshore chain to 15 fathoms. This will eliminate the possibility of getting its bight foul of the other anchor. Then when the tide begins running in the opposite direction, it will cause the ship to range ahead till the inshore anchor leads astern, after which the conditions governing the swinging will be the same as enumerated at the beginning of Section 3 in this chapter. After the ship swings with the tide, pay out to 30 fathoms on what is now the offshore chain. Since the inshore chain has already been shortened to 15 fathoms, the ship will be lying to her anchors in a manner similar to that on the opposite heading.

Or in the event there is a little stronger current running, give 30 fathoms of chain on the offshore anchor before dropping the inshore anchor and then pay out until they have 45 fathoms and 15 fathoms, respectively.

In this instance when the tide begins to turn, heave in 30 fathoms on the offshore chain, then, with the inshore chain leading astern, the conditions with regard to the swinging will again be the same as enumerated at the beginning of Section 3 of this chapter.

When anchoring in this manner, regardless of how much chain

is given to the offshore anchor, the inshore anchor should not be given more than about 15 fathoms. Reason: The steadying effect of the short scope is much more beneficial and essential than the holding effect of a slightly longer chain.

5. Preventing Anchors from Dragging

If the anchors start dragging, the reason probably will be that they broke away from the bottom when the flukes and shank became so balled up with mud that the anchors entirely lost their digging-in ability. The best remedy is to heave up and get them free of mud.

The most effective way to prevent the anchors from dragging is to be sure, when they are dropped, to let the chains pay out freely enough so as not to take a heavy strain; when the desired scope is out, use the ship's engine in order to cause the chains to come taut as gently as possible.

Chapter Three

Mooring

1. Causes of Ship's Breaking Adrift

In some narrow inland waterways the current is abnormally strong at times because of freshets. When this condition exists, if a ship is moored to a dock that is built parallel with, and along the edge of, the deep water, she will get the full force of the current; and in such cases it is extremely difficult to keep the ship from breaking adrift. Mooring in a manner which differs from the conventional will reduce this hazard to a minimum.

Of course, the conventional manner is to moor flat alongside the dock, either head to or stern to the current. For the sake of simplifying the illustration only head to the current will be considered.

A method similar to that which is used in preventing a ship at anchor from going broadside to the current, and then dragging, can be used if the ship is moored to a dock—but with even more certainty of satisfactory results. The conventional or—in this case—the wrong way to moor will be discussed first.

When an effort is made to keep the ship flat alongside the dock it sometimes happens that the bow gets off a trifle. Whenever this occurs, then each additional fraction of a degree the ship heads out causes the force of the current to get a little stronger on the inshore bow which, in turn, makes it much more difficult for it to be held, till finally the force of the current will, in all proba-

Figure 11. Ships moored in a narrow channel.

bility, become so strong that it will be impossible to hold the bow and it will consequently break adrift. It is needless to say what will next happen to the after lines. It might be worth while however to state that, after the bow gets off from the dock but before any of the forward lines let go, it rarely ever happens that any of the after lines carry away.

And even should the force of the current strike slightly heavier on the *off*shore bow, the ship will still have a considerable tendency to want to sheer *away* from the dock. This is because of the ship's location or position in the channel. Her stern is close to shoal water, on the dock side, consequently the suction causes her quarter to want to draw in.

This accounts for the fact that, when the bow gets off from the dock, there is very little probability of the after lines carrying away before the forward ones do.

2. Safeguards Against Ship's Breaking Adrift

There are certain precautions which can be taken to safeguard against a ship breaking adrift.

The after lines are helpful principally in a negative manner. That is to say they can do much more harm than good. In fact a ship would be just as well off (if she were moored, head to, in a heavy freshet) if there were no after lines out at all, except the breasts. In defense of this statement, a tug lashed up to a barge will be given as an illustration. The only after lines the tug has out are breast lines.

The relation of the ship to the wharf (when the ship is moored head to, in a strong current) is similar to that of the tug, when she is going full speed, to her barge. For the tug to hold on to her barge if their headings were exactly parallel would be very difficult at any time, and if the headway were great enough, it would be impossible. Only a slight divergence of their heading would increase, still more, the probability of their breaking adrift.

On the other hand they can easily be held together, at any speed, if their headings converge the proper amount. In the first case the pressure of the water between them is trying to force them apart. Whereas in the other instance the effect of the water helps to keep them together. The same principle holds true with regard to the ship and the wharf.

3. Mooring Lines

Now to go into detail about mooring. The after lines can easily be taken care of. Simply be sure that none have much strain on them—especially the stern and spring lines. The angle at which the ship should be headed toward the dock should be controlled by slacking off sufficiently on the stern breast lines.

With regard to the forward part of the ship, there must be out plenty of head lines and they must be especially good. But only slightly less important are the springs, because since the stern lines are to be left slack the function of the stern lines must be performed by the springs. Relative to the comment to be made about the breast lines it will be repeated that the bow back springs are exceedingly important. Therefore caution should be taken not to offset their beneficial effect by having the bow breasts lead wrong. Which is to say the breasts must not lead at all ahead but should tend, at least, slightly—but definitely—astern.

It might be well to go into still more detail about the location of the breast lines. If they were to lead ahead enough to help materially in relieving the strain on the bow lines they would then no longer really act as breasts. Or if they lead just slightly ahead, then if the back spring lines should render, the ship would surge —not only ahead but also away from the dock—till the breast lines were directly abeam.

"Between the lines" in this section, an anomaly has been running. It is this: The stronger the current runs, the stronger is the tendency of the ship to want to range ahead. This action on the part of the ship, however, can be accounted for. When the bow is forced offshore the strain on the head lines increases, consequently, if they do not part, the ship must range ahead. This should further emphasize the fact that the fitness of the bow back springs (no bow forward springs should be put out) and the proper lead of the (bow) breasts are of only slightly less importance than the head lines.

4. Mooring Position

The position in which it is desired to have the ship moored will now be considered. The after breast lines should be slacked sufficiently to allow the stern to go away from the dock enough to cause a slight preponderance of the current to strike the offshore bow. (It has previously been pointed out that the stern and stern spring lines should be left slack.) This will cause the inshore bow to take a little weight on the dock. Then with the bow spring and breast lines tight the ship most surely will lie satisfactorily.

5. Working with the Elements

The comments in this chapter might serve as a means of revealing a secret in regard to successful ship-handling. It is this: A ship can be much more successfully and safely handled by taking advantage of, and cooperating with, the elements to the fullest extent—instead of disregarding and working against them. In fact this is almost a requisite to successful handling.

Chapter Four

Best Trim for Maneuvering

1. TRIMMING A DEEP LOADED SHIP

In Chapter II it was pointed out that a ship could lie against a mud bank without sustaining damage. It is likewise true that when a ship is under way she may drag over a silt, or even a soft mud bottom without being damaged; and in order to load a full cargo in some ports, this too is sometimes a necessary practice.

A ship that is quite a few inches in the mud will make headway but she will not answer her rudder satisfactorily—if she answers at all—unless she is trimmed so as to cope with existing conditions. However, if properly trimmed, a deep loaded ship a few inches *in* the mud will generally handle *better* than she would if she were just afloat, or just clear of the bottom.

This is true because, almost without exception, a deep loaded ship just clear of the bottom is very wild. On the other hand suppose that with a slack tide, a head tide, or a cross current to be encountered on the bar or en route, a loaded ship, under way, is 6 inches by the head, and in this trim her forefoot is dragging 3 inches in the mud, her stern 3 inches clear of the bottom.

The fact that the ship is dragging in the mud—instead of being a handicap—is a decided advantage. In regard to swinging, her bow is almost as effectively controlled by the mud as hinges control the pivoting end of a door.

But with a fair tide and the same mean draft, the ship should have a 6 inch drag. This would put her stern 3 inches in the mud.

Naturally, she would be sluggish in answering her rudder. If there were sharp turns, or if at times the current had to be gotten quite a bit on the side, then having the assistance of a tug on a hawser would be about the most satisfactory way to cope with the situation.

Ordinarily, in a narrow channel, it is quite a problem to get the way off of a deep loaded ship if she is wild. However, if she is in

Figure 12. In a good trim for maneuvering.

the mud—and in the proper trim—she is not only apt to be easy to keep steady but, furthermore, she will very quickly lose headway if the engine is stopped.

2. MAKING SHARP TURNS

Next suppose that, between where the ship is loading a full cargo and the open sea, the channel is deep enough so that she will be afloat, but that there are turns so sharp that in what is generally recognized as the proper trim, *i.e.*, quite a few inches by the stern, the ship does not have sufficient rudder power to make her swing fast enough to make the turns. (See Frontispiece, Chart A.)

She can be made to swing considerably faster by putting her 6 or more inches by the head. In this trim she will no doubt be wild, but not too wild to be kept under control.

3. Trimming a Ship in Ballast

On the other hand when a ship is light, or in ballast, she is under the best all-around control if she *is* decidedly by the stern. (See Figure 24.)

A tanker will be used for the illustrations since she can easily be put in almost any desired trim; and a contrast will be made between two extremes in trim. Suppose there is a strong wind blowing, and that at 20 feet the tip of the propeller projects slightly above the water and at 14 feet the hub is just submerged.

With a mean draft of 12 feet it would, on the whole, be much better to have her drawing only 4 feet forward and 20 feet aft than (with the same mean draft) to have her 10 feet forward and 14 feet aft.

The first trim has only one serious fault, her bow will be bad about going to leeward in case it is necessary to let the ship lose considerable headway[1]; and her bow will be extremely bad about falling off if it should be necessary to work the engine astern.

However, by putting her so much by the stern and thereby creating one *un*favorable condition, the following disadvantages are eliminated and equivalent advantages are gained:

1. (a) Since she is practically flat bottomed, the modern ship makes a great deal of leeway when on an even keel because she rests on the flat part of her hull.

---

[1] How a ship might be held broadside to the wind when she has only slight headway will be found in Situation 10 b, Chapter VI.

(b) When she is decidedly by the stern, the leeway is lessened because she rests more on the sharp after part which has the same effect as the keel of a sailing vessel or the centerboard of a sail boat.

2. (a) When the hub is only slightly submerged, the blades on the top side do practically nothing to offset the effect of the pitch of the blades at the bottom. In addition, a great deal of the rudder

Figure 13. About half of this ship's propeller is out of water; consequently, after passing another ship port to port, full right rudder could not prevent her from sheering across the canal and striking her port bank.

is above water which makes this portion of no benefit in steering. Hence it is apt to take from 7 to 10 degrees of right rudder to keep the ship steady when she has full headway. With the ship dead in the water, her bow might go to port or, to be more exact, her stern might go to starboard even against full right rudder, when the engine is first worked full speed ahead. (See Figures 13 and 14.)

(b) With the propeller nearly submerged, there is almost a maximum force of wheel water, and there is a large rudder area for the wheel water to strike against, thereby achieving very effective rudder power.

3. (a) With the hub just submerged, the propeller is extremely *in*effective in killing the headway when worked full speed astern.

Another fault is that with the hub almost out of water, when the engine is backed, the ship's stern will swing to port a great deal. This makes it very difficult and hazardous to stop by backing.

Figure 14. Ship is "jacked."

(b) When the propeller is nearly submerged, it is exceedingly effective in killing the headway when worked full speed astern.

Of course, on a mean draft of 12 feet the ship would have in very little ballast, if any at all. With regard to ballast, the gist of these remarks is this: The ship will be kept in much the best trim if, when taking in ballast, the stern is kept deep enough so that the propeller stays entirely submerged, or nearly so.

4. IMPORTANCE OF APPROPRIATE TRIMMING

By again resorting to the theory that ships have life, this comparison can be made:

When hypnotized a person can be made to do things, and has the ability to withstand ordeals, that are entirely beyond his normal powers. In the same way, a ship, when she is abnormally but appropriately trimmed, can be made to do things she is otherwise incapable of doing. When she is especially trimmed for the difficulties that are to be encountered, she can often be made to overcome them; whereas, were she normally or conventionally trimmed, it would be impossible for her to cope with the same conditions successfully.

5. NAVIGATING IN A DREDGED CHANNEL THAT IS IN OPEN WATER

There are dredged channels in open water where the prevailing current runs, roughly, at right angles to the channel's direction. When a ship is navigating such a channel, if she is dragging over the bottom or is slightly in the mud, the only proper trim is for her to be a few inches by the head. Such a trim will enable her to hold up against the crosscurrent much more readily.

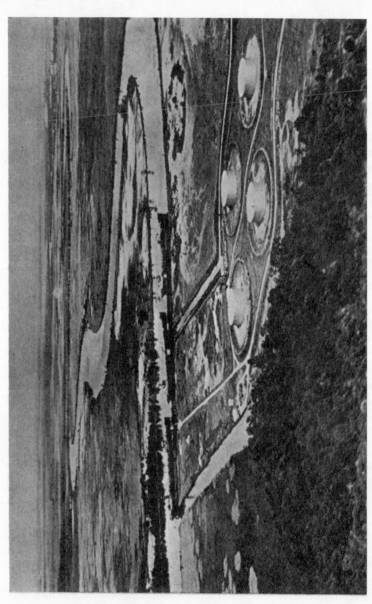

Figure 15. Tankers loading at a river terminal. (See Figures 16 and 17.)

Chapter Five

Using Tugs Advantageously

1. Tug on a Hawser Getting Away from Dock

An expression frequently heard during the days of sail was: "Different ships, different long-splices." So today: In different channels—or harbors—there is enough dissimilarity in conditions to bring about different customs, or practices, with regard to the use of tugs.

First a tug assisting a deep loaded ship through a narrow and crooked channel will be considered. To be more explicit, with the ship deep loaded, it will be assumed she is only clearing the bottom by inches most of the time. Under these circumstances she will steer poorly because of "smelling" both the bottom and the banks, and she is also capable of creating about the maximum degree of disturbance in the water when passing other vessels.

To make it easier to visualize the conditions, we will have her sail from the dock shown in Figures 15 and 16. As the picture shows, there are also two other ships moored at this dock; the one to get under way is in the middle. Assume that the tide will be slack.

Keep out a doubled-up stern line leading from the starboard quarter. Let go everything else, aft. Forward, take in everything except a short head line leading from the starboard bow.

Give the tug about 200 feet of hawser from the port bow chock; have her pull off in a direction about 20 degrees forward of the

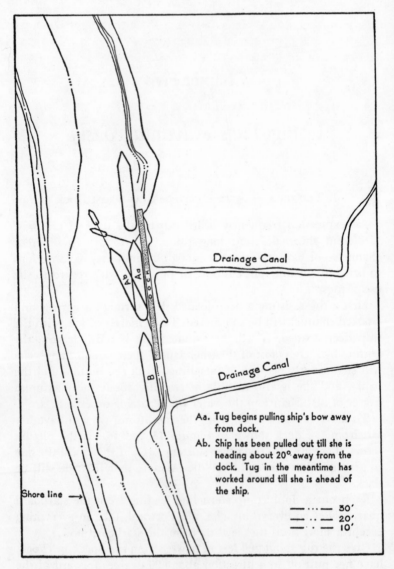

Drainage Canal

Drainage Canal

Aa. Tug begins pulling ship's bow away from dock.

Ab. Ship has been pulled out till she is heading about 20° away from the dock. Tug in the meantime has worked around till she is ahead of the ship.

Shore line →

— ··· — 30'
— ·· — 20'
— · — 10'

Figure 16. (See Figure 15.)

beam. As soon as a strain comes on the hawser the stern lines will come tight; also, ordinarily, the quarter would slap heavily against the dock, however the head line coming tight prevents this from happening.

The tug must head out so nearly abeam because a loaded ship so close to the bottom, or possibly sometimes slightly grazing the bottom, when being pulled broadside—especially with one end made fast—is a very dead weight. It will therefore need practically all of the tug's power to pull her bow off sufficiently.

After both stern and head lines have a strain on them and the ship's quarter is resting firmly against the dock, surge the head line. In addition to letting the bow swing out it will also allow the quarter (farther aft) to keep—gently—coming in, which is to say, it will *prevent* the quarter from taking too heavily.

As the bow swings out have the tug gradually work around— being careful that she does not come around too quickly—on a right rudder so as to be directly ahead of the ship by the time the ship is heading out, roughly, 20 degrees.

Now unless judgment should happen to be perfectly accurate in getting the tug directly ahead of the ship at the proper time, there is danger of the ship's bow being pulled out much more than is desired, thereby causing her counter to get over the top of the dock which might endanger the rudder and propeller. These potential dangers are entirely eliminated by properly checking or holding the bow line, if necessary.

After the ship's bow is out the desired amount, and the tug is pulling directly ahead of the ship, let the tug continue pulling in this direction, and take in the bow line. Remember there are out two stern lines leading from the starboard quarter, and they naturally have a heavy strain on them.

These two lines are now serving in a dual capacity: In addition to being stern lines, they are also acting as *offshore* breasts, and are causing the stern to go *away* from the dock. (See Figure 17.) When the quarter gets sufficiently clear of the dock, both stern

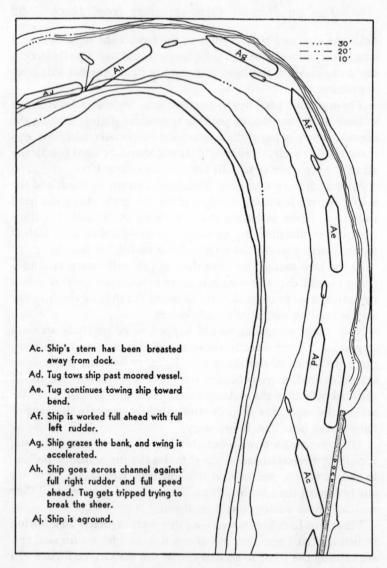

Ac. Ship's stern has been breasted away from dock.

Ad. Tug tows ship past moored vessel.

Ae. Tug continues towing ship toward bend.

Af. Ship is worked full ahead with full left rudder.

Ag. Ship grazes the bank, and swing is accelerated.

Ah. Ship goes across channel against full right rudder and full speed ahead. Tug gets tripped trying to break the sheer.

Aj. Ship is aground.

Figure 17. (See Figure 15.)

lines will be taken in; the tug has continued, in the meantime, to pull straight ahead. In all probability the propeller can be kept motionless while the stern lines are being hove in, since the tug is pulling the ship in a safe direction. However, if the necessity should arise, the propeller can be worked in ahead motion without danger of the lines getting in it, since they will be leading astern—the tug's pulling having given the ship headway.

Even after the stern lines have been hove in it still is important to keep the propeller motionless, if possible, because the ship that is moored ahead of where our ship was moored, will be disturbed by the wheel water if the propeller is worked, while it is anywhere near abreast of the moored ship.

(This method of getting under way could also be used with a light ship even though there were a strong beam wind blowing on the dock, because the stern lines would still breast the stern off.)

A conventional critic of these maneuvers might say: The ship can be gotten away from the dock without taking all these precautions or without going to all of this trouble.

It will be readily agreed that all of the mooring lines could have been let go, and the ship could still be gotten away from the dock. However, to do so, her quarter would almost certainly have taken quite heavily on the dock. Next, the propeller would, necessarily, have had to be worked astern occasionally, while the bow was being pulled out. This would cause her quarter to come against the dock, probably bounce off a little and then come against it again. While this was happening, the quarter would also be dragging ahead and astern along the edge of the dock—depending on the working of the engine; later, the propeller and rudder might be endangered. In addition to this, the wheel water would no doubt disturb, at least slightly, the ship moored so close astern. Then after the head was gotten out sufficiently, the suction that had been created by the working of the propeller (owing to the fact that the dock is so close to the shore line) would have a tendency to hold the stern alongside of the dock. Consequently, when starting ahead, the quarter would be strongly inclined to drag along the dock and this, in turn, would cause the bow to head for the opposite side of the channel. (See Section 9, Chapter I.) To prevent the ship from going too far toward the opposite side of the channel the propeller would have to be worked almost continuously—with the rudder full right—while passing the ship that is moored ahead of where our ship was moored. This most surely would cause the moored ship to range ahead and astern on her moorings.

2. Tug on a Hawser Making a Sharp Bend

By the time our ship gets comfortably clear of the ship which is moored to the dock and which she has just passed, she must be gotten in the proper position to make a bend where the direction of the river changes about 90 degrees to the left in approximately five ship lengths.

After helping the ship away from the dock the tug on a hawser is no longer where she can render the most effective assistance. However, this is the simplest way to use her as well as the manner in which, generally speaking, she can best expedite the ship's passage through the channel. Furthermore, the bank of this bend is nearly straight up and down (see Figure 17) and since such a bend enables a ship to swing more sharply than would otherwise be possible, besides making it least likely that she will run aground in the bend, the tug is left on a hawser.

When the bend has been reached, in starting to make it, or any similar bend, it is extremely improbable that steerageway alone (which, of course, includes working the engine at various speeds) could create enough of a swing. (It will be recalled that this is a deep loaded ship close to the bottom, and these conditions make her very sluggish about answering her rudder.) The necessary turn can be accomplished only when suction, also, is utilized to the fullest possible extent; and in this instance, if suction is made use of bow wave automatically becomes quite a contributing factor. Also of help is a tug on a hawser. In other words, if all of the above forces are used in coordination with steerageway, the necessary swing will be most certain of accomplishment. If these factors are not used in coordination, it is very improbable that the swing can be made.

However, of this contributing trio the tug is—or, to express it more accurately—the tug is apt, from necessity, to be made the least important; because the tug, on a hawser, can render enough help to be of importance only as long as the ship has very little headway, or is dead in the water. The reason for this is twofold. First, only when the ship is going slow is it possible for the tug to go enough faster than the ship to keep a heavy strain on the hawser; second, when the ship has much headway, if the tug (having in mind the American type of tug which has her towing bitts well aft) gets over enough to affect the ship's swinging appreciably—and especially if she gets over to break a sheer— there is danger of the tug getting "tripped."

To amplify on the importance of the tug: It is sometimes true that a tug is the extra factor which enables a ship to make a bend. Nevertheless, in many instances, it would be possible for a loaded ship as large as the one under consideration to make the bend that is being discussed without the assistance of a tug. But as the purpose of this chapter, primarily, is to consider the use of tugs in various ways, we will first make the bend with a tug on a hawser.

As the bend is being approached, and all during the time it is being made, the tug should stay over toward the point as much as she can safely do so without the risk of getting tripped. (The less the ship's headway, the less is the danger of the tug tripping.)

As for the ship, when she is approaching the bend, the tug's pulling will enable her to maintain as much headway as it is advisable to have; so if the ship will answer her rudder with the engine stopped, this is preferable; and if she will not, only give the ship a kick ahead when required. The tug is pulling toward the point, but in spite of this fact the ship will be able to head toward the bend as much as is desired. The desired distance away from the bank, while approaching the bend, generally is about as close as the ship will stay with the rudder hard over toward the bank (in this case full right) and the engine stopped, or with a kick ahead occasionally.

If the ship is approaching in this manner, when it is time to make the bend, the following things—in coordination—will all tend to help her to swing fast enough to make it: First, suction (because her stern already is strongly inclined to want to draw in); second, bow wave (because her bow is close enough in—and the bank is near enough straight up and down—to create a heavy cushion which will force the bow offshore); third, the tug (because she is in the proper position, and the ship is going slow enough to enable her to render very effective help); fourth, engine (slow ahead); fifth, rudder (hard over—full left in this case).

Working the engine slow ahead will decrease the help derived from the tug's pulling, but will increase the beneficial effect of the rudder, suction, and bow wave; and these three are by far the most essential. Then if the ship does not swing fast enough and consequently keeps getting "deeper" into the bend—and in all probability this is what will happen—the thing to do is give her not half, but full, speed ahead. The maximum swing that can be created is needed instantly, therefore too much time would be lost if half speed were first given. This will almost invariably get the desired result, which is to finish making the bend. However in this instance, just before the bend is completed her bow grazes along the slope of the bank. (See Figure 17.)

This accelerates the swing in spite of the fact that we are now about ready to want to—or rather we soon will have to—steady up. Consequently the rudder is quickly eased to amidships and then put full right (in this case). Nevertheless with the tug pulling her over, the bow wave—at first—forcing the bow out, and suction drawing the stern in, the ship keeps swinging till she heads for the opposite side.

The engine is kept full speed ahead because even though, theoretically, the ship should back to port and break the sheer,

Figure 18. This tug got "tripped."

in reality, this backing would only aggravate the sheer. Consequently, it would not merely cause the ship to go aground but she would be almost certain to go crosswise of the channel, and if she did, the rudder and propeller would be endangered.

Therefore working the engine full speed ahead with full right rudder is the best thing that can be done under the circumstances. However this is not sufficient as she keeps heading diagonally across the channel until it is too late for her to recover completely. In the meantime the tug having worked around (on the hawser, while pulling full speed) till she is well on the starboard bow, hauls over a little more so as to render the maximum amount of assistance when it is seen that the ship will quite likely run aground. The result is that the tug gets tripped, but she lets go of the hawser soon enough to keep from being drawn stern first against the ship's side.

These efforts did not prevent a grounding. Nevertheless they were the proper things to do since they caused the mishap to be the least disastrous, because when the ship took the bottom she had been gotten nearly parallel with the edge of the channel (in fact if she could have been headed out a trifle more the grounding would not have occurred) with the result that she brought up much more gently than she otherwise would have done.

3. Tug on Bow Getting Away from Dock

By now the ship which, in Figures 15 and 16, was lying farthest astern is ready to sail. Since the one that just sailed previously is now aground; and furthermore, since the two ships are similar in size, rudder power, draft, etc., there would be a serious likelihood of this ship performing the same as her predecessor—if she were handled in a similar manner. But now, if she were to act the same way, instead of there being simply a grounding, there would be a collision. Therefore special precaution will be taken to prevent this from happening. It will again be assumed the tide is slack.

The tug on a hawser would serve satisfactorily for getting away from the dock. However, she will be wanted alongside, on the port bow, to make the bend; consequently she will be used on the port bow also in getting away from the dock.

Let the tug put out these lines: one *short* bow line—leading ahead—to the break of the forecastlehead (or to the chock nearest to it on the main deck); another bow line—leading aft—to a chock in the neighborhood of the fore rigging; a stern line leading to a chock just forward of the bridge. (Made fast in this manner the tug's stem—or to be more correct, her bow-pudding—will be able to come against the ship's side slightly abaft the forecastle-head.)

Then the ship can take in everything aft; and take in everything forward except a back spring line and a breast line leading, preferably, through the starboard bow chock—so as to get the most leverage as well as to enable the bow to be hove in the most. Heave a strain on the breast line. As this is being done, let the tug work ahead on a right rudder—and while doing so slack away on her stern line—until the tug is about at right angles to the ship. When the tug gets at right angles to the ship hold the tug's stern line.

The tug in so maneuvering will be shoving the bow in alongside the dock; and the heaving on the breast line will be working toward the same end. The outcome of these two actions will be that the ship's stern will swing away from the dock.

[Right here an illustration of suction predominating over rudder power will be sandwiched in.

Suppose with the foregoing ship, when getting away from the dock, the bow breast and spring, and the tug were used the same as just described. As an additional help, the rudder is put full right and the engine worked slow ahead.

A glance at Figure 16 will show the stern of Ship B is jam up against shoal water; furthermore the contour of the edge of the channel is such as to create very powerful suction. Consequently not only will slow ahead on a full right rudder fail to help swing the stern away from the bank but, it will actually *prevent* the stern from going out.]

Therefore when the ship's stern has been swung out probably about 20 degrees without using the propeller so as to avoid creating suction, avast heaving and let go everything on the dock; stop the tug; go back on the ship's engine enough to cause her to go astern about half a ship length. While so doing she can be kept in the desired heading—or to be more explicit, she can be steered—by working the tug ahead or astern, if necessary, since the tug will be lying at right angles to the ship.

After going astern about a half ship length or so, the ship's bow can then be pulled sufficiently far out into the channel by backing on the tug. In letting the tug pull the ship's bow out in this manner, enough patience must be exercised to allow the tug sufficient time to pull the ship's bow out the required amount before the ship gathers much, or any, headway—because, after the ship has a little momentum, the tug will fall alongside; after which she will be of very little more help in pulling the bow out.

When all clear, and headway has been gathered, the engine can probably be kept stopped while abreast of the ship moored at the opposite end of the dock, as the tug on the bow can quite likely prevent a sheer.

4. Tug on Bow Making a Sharp Bend

The ship will now be made to approach the turn (with the tug alongside on the port bow) from a position which might seem to contradict many of the statements that have previously been made, since suction will, apparently, be disregarded—in fact it might even seem as though suction were being defied. Because in approaching the turn, not the bend, but the point, side of the channel will be favored; also the headway will be no more than dead slow.

Next assume the turn has been arrived at in the manner described above.

Just a little while ago, when this particular ship was being gotten away from the dock, it was pointed out that after the ship had headway enough to cause the tug to fall alongside, the tug could no longer be of much assistance in pulling the ship's bow toward her. With this statement fresh in the reader's mind, he might ask, quite naturally: Without the help of suction, without much headway, and without material help from the tug, what is there left that can cause the ship to swing fast enough to negotiate this sharp turn?

An explanation must be given to account for (1) *why* it is possible to accomplish this contrary or conflicting maneuver; and also (2) *why* it is necessary to favor the point side of the channel. It will be recalled that throughout the book this fact has been stressed: The less the headway, the less the suction. In approaching the turn—on the point side—and in making the turn, this "axiom" will be heeded.

This axiom also helps account for the first *why*: Why the swing is possible in spite of the fact that it is started from the point side of the channel. A fuller explanation will be found in Section 9, Chapter I, where it says—in effect: (a) The slower the headway, the weaker the suction. (b) The farther away from shoal water (which in this case happens to be the point), the weaker the suction.

Now, the tug's backing is such a powerful factor in enabling rudder power to predominate over suction that, with its contributing influence, the ship will—it is quite safe to say—without exception, respond to her rudder; and as the ship frees herself from the retarding effect of the bank's suction, she will swing faster.

Next, to answer the second *why*: In spite of the fact that when leaving the dock the tug's assistance could no longer be of consequence, after the ship gathered enough headway to cause the tug to fall flat alongside of the ship—she nevertheless plays an all-important role in this particular case, in helping the ship make the swing. Because with the ship working ahead slow, the tug's backing—even though the tug is lying flat alongside of the ship—acts practically the same as the anchor (port in this case) leading astern would act in retarding the ship's headway. The result is that the bow is kept nearly stationary while the wheel water against full left rudder forces the stern toward the bend. Therefore in order to keep from getting too deep in the bend, or in other words, in order to have sufficient swinging room, the turn must be started on the point side of the channel.

(This explanation also should serve to tell why, after the ship gathered headway, the tug's assistance would be inadequate in helping the ship get clear of the dock.)

It has been implied and also frequently stated that the ship's headway is an influence adverse to the tug's getting in the most favorable position with regard to rendering effective help. Conversely, just before it has been completely killed, headway will become so impotent that its adverse effect will be overcome by a favorable factor, the tug's *short* bow line that she is backing on. Being short, it acts as a breast line and—when the ship's momentum has died down sufficiently—will cause the tug's stem to come alongside of the ship; this in turn throws the tug's stern away from the ship. In this position the tug is (1) still pulling back on the ship; (2) deflecting the ship's bow in the desired direction; (3) somewhat broadside to the ship's headway and thereby acting as a drag which is an additional factor in helping to kill the ship's momentum; (4) helping to deflect, by this dragging effect, the ship's bow in the desired direction.

Probably the reader has had in mind another factor that will help throw the tug's stern out—the tug on the port bow (with a right-handed propeller) will back to port. This feature has intentionally been neglected until now with the hope that by so doing attention might, most emphatically, be called to a mistake that is committed by almost everyone when first starting to handle craft of any kind. Some men even with years of experience are guilty of this mistake of relying or depending too much on theory. This is especially true in anticipating (1) that a right-handed, single-screw ship will always back to port, or swing her head to starboard; (2) that a twin-screw ship will always swing her head toward the side of the backing propeller. There are innumerable things that might cause either of these ships to fail to act in the anticipated manner.

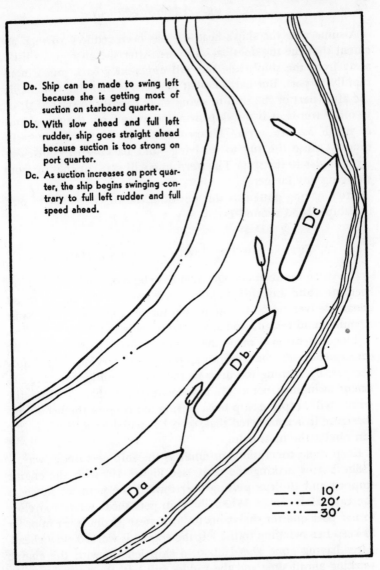

Da. Ship can be made to swing left because she is getting most of suction on starboard quarter.

Db. With slow ahead and full left rudder, ship goes straight ahead because suction is too strong on port quarter.

Dc. As suction increases on port quarter, the ship begins swinging contrary to full left rudder and full speed ahead.

—·— 10'
—··— 20'
—···— 30'

Figure 19

71

Assume now the ship's headway has been reduced to such an extent that the tug does back to port. After she once gets a little away from the ship's side she will *apparently* back much more rapidly to port. But part of what happens is that she will enable the after part of the ship to swing more rapidly to starboard; or in other words, it is the ship swinging away from the tug almost as much as vice versa. This combination of movements will quickly cause the tug to be lying—and backing of course—at right angles to the ship. The stern line will prevent the tug from swinging any farther.

After having gotten in this position, the tug is bound to pull the ship's head around eventually.

5. Cutting the Point with a Tug on a Hawser

It will be assumed enough time has elapsed, since the ship (in Sections 1 and 2 of this chapter) ran ashore, to enable her to get afloat; deliver her cargo at its destination; return to the same terminal, and reload. And again she is ready to sail.

The contention is made that: (1) the effect of suction is of no consequence; (2) the ship ran ashore on the previous trip simply because, by keeping too deep in the bend, she did not have sufficient swinging room; (3) it is maintained that "cutting the point" will keep the ship from getting too deep in the bend. Furthermore it is considered that, on a hawser, the tug is where she can render the most help.

Keep these conclusions in mind as the ship gets under way.

She begins making the turn (see Figure 19) with the engine stopped and the tug pulling over toward the point as much as she can safely do so. When the ship gets shoal water too close to her port quarter she wants to "run away" from it, so in order to keep her swinging to the left the engine is worked slow ahead. After having gone ahead about a ship length, with the engine working ahead slow and the rudder full left, she again quits an-

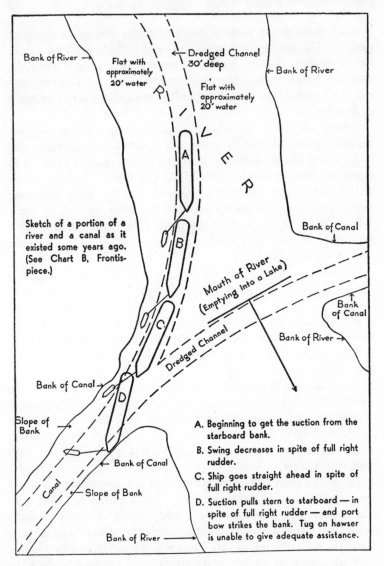

Bank of River

Flat with approximately 20' water

Dredged Channel 30' deep

Bank of River

Flat with approximately 20' water

R I V E R

A

B

Bank of Canal

Sketch of a portion of a river and a canal as it existed some years ago. (See Chart B, Frontispiece.)

Mouth of River (Emptying Into a Lake)

Bank of Canal

C

Dredged Channel

Bank of River

Bank of Canal

D

Slope of Bank

Bank of Canal

Canal

Slope of Bank

Bank of River

A. Beginning to get the suction from the starboard bank.

B. Swing decreases in spite of full right rudder.

C. Ship goes straight ahead in spite of full right rudder.

D. Suction pulls stern to starboard — in spite of full right rudder — and port bow strikes the bank. Tug on hawser is unable to give adequate assistance.

Figure 20

swering because the suction has gotten too strong on the port quarter. The engine is therefore worked full ahead. This causes her to answer, slightly, for about another ship length when she once more steadies up. (See Section 9, Chapter I.) The tug, during the interval, has constantly pulled toward the point as much as possible.

While this has been taking place the ship has been—quite rapidly—going diagonally across the channel. Consequently, she soon strikes the bank of the bend, and near enough head on to cause her bow to become grounded. The tide is slack, nevertheless, her headway has created a swell that has been following astern and soon catches up and lifts the after part of the ship, forcing it onto the shoal on the point side of the channel. (See Section 8, Chapter I.) Therefore the ship is aground fore and aft, and she is also "jacked."

6. Disadvantages of Having Tug on the Bow

It is possible the three foregoing illustrations might convey the impression that the only proper way to make a sharp bend with a deep loaded ship is to have the tug alongside, on the bow—on the *point* side.

It is true that by adopting this procedure a bend can very often be negotiated, when the tug's assistance in any other manner would be inadequate. However this method, too, has disadvantages, namely: loss of time to the ship; danger to the tug; much extra maneuvering for the tug, and extra work for both tug's and ship's crew.

In reply to the first, it might be said the loss of time is of no consequence if it prevents a mishap. But a glance at Chart A in the Frontispiece will show eight sharp bends in about as many miles. Each sharp bend will cause a delay of about 15 or 20 minutes; so, maneuvering in this manner can quickly run into hours.

With regard to the tug being in danger—notwithstanding the fact that she can get tripped when on a hawser—the danger is

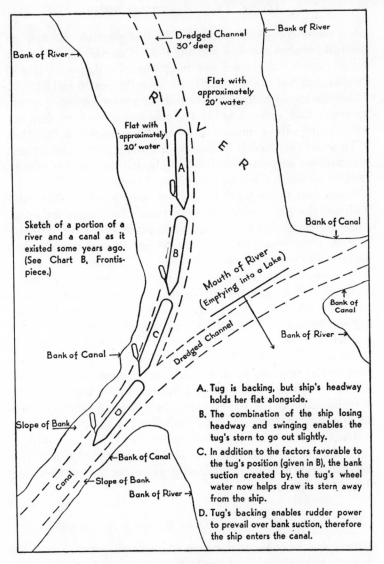

Dredged Channel
30' deep

← Bank of River

Bank of River →

Flat with
approximately
20' water

Flat with
approximately
20' water

R
I
V
E
R

A

B

Sketch of a portion of a
river and a canal as it
existed some years ago.
(See Chart B, Frontis-
piece.)

Bank of Canal

Mouth of River
(Emptying into a Lake)

Bank of Canal

C

Dredged Channel

Bank of River →

Bank of Canal ←

Slope of Bank

D

←Bank of Canal

←Slope of Bank

Canal

Bank of River →

A. Tug is backing, but ship's headway
   holds her flat alongside.
B. The combination of the ship losing
   headway and swinging enables the
   tug's stern to go out slightly.
C. In addition to the factors favorable to
   the tug's position (given in B), the bank
   suction created by the tug's wheel
   water now helps draw its stern away
   from the ship.
D. Tug's backing enables rudder power
   to prevail over bank suction, therefore
   the ship enters the canal.

Figure 21

75

more imminent when alongside. In this position she can get jammed between the ship and the bank. Generally speaking the tug is perfectly safe from jamming when on the point side of the channel, but not necessarily so. (See Figures 20 and 21.)

But the loss of time is not the only disadvantage. Since, in any waterway, each succeeding bend almost invariably turns contrariwise, the tug will be constantly shifting from one bow to the other.

To avoid the trouble of shifting from one side to the other it is sometimes advocated that the tug be left on the port bow regardless of which direction the channel turns.

When next to the bend, aside from being in a very vulnerable position, the tug is where she can render practically no worthwhile assistance. If the ship has much headway the tug is unable to work up to where she can shove *in* on the ship to a sufficient degree; but instead can only shove ahead—an undesirable action. And if the ship's headway is only reduced sufficiently to enable a tug which has exceptionally good rudder power to work up to where she is nearly at right angles to the ship's heading, her pushing will be materially offset by the dragging effect caused by the tug being broadside to the direction in which the ship is making headway. (See Figure 22.) In other words, the effect that is desired is just opposite to that which was wanted in Section 4 of this chapter. Only when the ship is dead in the water, will this dragging effect of the tug be entirely eliminated; however it will be nominal, or inconsequential, when there is slight headway.

The foregoing can be summed up by saying: It is preferable to keep the tug on a hawser, instead of on the bow, if it can be reasonably anticipated that the ship will make the bend by using the tug in this manner.

7. Making a Bend Where Deep Water Is Alongside Point

Next will be considered a turn where the deepest water is not in the bend—where it generally is—but alongside of the point. Such a turn is very difficult for a loaded ship to negotiate, be-

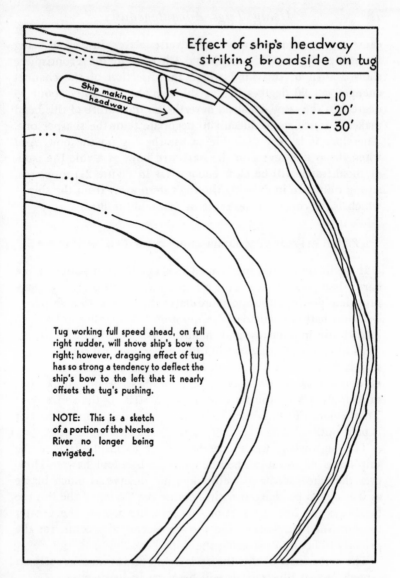

Effect of ship's headway
striking broadside on tug

Ship making headway

—— · —— 10'
—— · · —— 20'
—— · · · —— 30'

Tug working full speed ahead, on full
right rudder, will shove ship's bow to
right; however, dragging effect of tug
has so strong a tendency to deflect the
ship's bow to the left that it nearly
offsets the tug's pushing.

NOTE: This is a sketch
of a portion of the Neches
River no longer being
navigated.

Figure 22

77

cause suction and bow wave are adverse factors, instead of being favorable. Figures 20 and 21 and Chart B in the Frontispiece show a turn of this kind where the direction of the channel changes not 90 degrees in five ship lengths, but only about 55 degrees in the same distance; nevertheless the nature of this bend makes it much more difficult to negotiate than the sharper one. Therefore it is very desirable to use the tug on the bow. And when she is used even on the starboard bow, as a rule the bank or shoal water will be close enough (as in Figure 21) to exert a strong influence in drawing the tug's stern away from the ship—which is, of course, a desirable or favorable influence.

8. Ill Effects to a Loaded Ship from Tug on Hawser

If medicine is improperly used it is apt to do a patient more harm than good. Likewise, if a tug is used improperly—or inappropriately—she might do more harm than good, to a ship.

The situation particularly in question is a tug ahead of a deep loaded ship in a narrow and shallow canal. The men who handle ships in such waterways are in quite general accord that a loaded ship is "wilder" with a tug on a hawser. But there is a difference of opinion as to what causes the wildness. Many think it is caused entirely by the tug's wheel water striking the ship's bow. To alleviate this unfavorable factor, a very long scope of hawser is paid out.

The tug's wheel water does have some harmful effect on the ship's steering and it can best be remedied by a long hawser. However the wheel water probably does not deserve as much blame as it is apt to be charged with; because the "axiom," the less the headway; the less the suction—or in other words, the greater the headway; the greater the suction—seems to account for the primary difficulty in steering the ship.

The correctness of this theory is by no means unanimously accepted, so two illustrations will be given in its defense.

First, with a bad steering ship just slightly clear of the bottom, in a narrow canal, rudder power will often predominate over suction when the ship is making only dead slow speed; whereas if she goes any faster than this, she will go wild. Consequently a tug on a hawser—even though only working slow—will increase the ship's headway or speed—when the ship's engine is working so slow—and this slight additional speed caused by the tug's pulling will create too much suction.

Second, without a tug on a hawser, a ship making, say, three knots under her own power *alone* will steer better than she would if her own power were creating a speed of only two knots and, say, something running along the shore and towing on a hawser —such as an electric mule—were creating one additional knot of speed. In the latter instance there would be no tug's wheel water disturbance. Nevertheless, the ship would steer decidedly better if her engine power *alone* were causing the three-knot speed. Reason: There will be a stronger force of wheel water against the ship's rudder.

In contradiction of the above statements it might be said that such a ship will sometimes go for miles without sheering, with the ship's engine working full speed; and innumerable instances can be cited to uphold this statement. The answer to this contention is found in Section 1, Chapter IV, where it says,

". . . a deep loaded ship a few inches *in* the mud will generally handle *better* than she would if she were just afloat, or just clear of the bottom. . . . The fact that the ship is dragging in the mud—instead of being a handicap—is a decided advantage.

But, it might be contended, this ship was supposed to be afloat. True. However a ship just afloat, while dead in the water, will often "squat" enough—when the engine is worked full speed— to cause her to drag heavily on the bottom.

To further substantiate the opinion that the wheel water from the tug on a long scope of hawser is not a serious disturbance, the following actual narration will be given:

The ship shown in Figure 23 is a twin-screw motor ship. When her engines were worked as slow as possible—either with or without a tug on a hawser—she would, after going a few ship lengths, gather too much headway to be kept under control in a narrow canal.

On the other hand, by lashing a tug up on the quarter and then by having another tug on a hawser—and not working the ship's engines at all—she could be kept under control. However, if—even with the assistance of the two tugs—the ship's engines were worked ahead a few minutes, the ship would go wild.

Figure 23. This ship is navigating a narrow and shallow canal by using one tug lashed up on the quarter, and another tug on a hawser.

Experience with many other similar ships has been the same.

Thus it would seem, it is the extra *speed* created by the pulling of the tug on a hawser which causes the ship to go wild, rather than the tug's wheel water.

9. Help to a Light Ship from Tug on Hawser

Although a tug on a hawser is quite apt to be an annoyance to a loaded ship when she is in a narrow and shallow canal, on the other hand, a tug will have very little if any bad effect on a light ship, especially one such as a tanker, if she is well down by the stern and drawing very little forward. (See the tanker in Figure 24.)

In this trim, the tug's pulling—with the ship's engine stopped most of the time—will not create enough headway to cause too much suction.[1] Consequently the tug on a hawser can be made to control the bow while the ship's rudder and propeller are controlling the stern.

Figure 24. This ship is in a good trim for navigating a narrow canal.

The tug on the hawser can render valuable assistance (hawser leading to the tug can be seen).

For example, if it should be necessary, the ship's headway can be killed entirely in this way: The tug gets over close to the port bank—while, at the same time, the ship is maneuvered close to the starboard bank; the ship can be backed, and while doing so she can be kept parallel with the channel, and thereby stopped.

[1] The statement is made in this manner in order to bring out most clearly the illustration. In actual practice, unless a ship is extremely "bad," she can be worked ahead dead slow, continuously.

Likewise when a *light* ship is making sharp bends in a river, the proper place for a tug is on a hawser, because with the bow of the ship having so little hold in the water, the tug can pull the ship's bow in the desired direction—without danger of the tug's getting tripped. One proviso: For the tug's pulling to have the necessary effect, the ship must not have too much headway. Stating it another way: The less headway the ship has, the more beneficial the tug's pulling will be.

The contrast in the effect of a tug on a hawser, when ahead of a light ship and when ahead of a loaded ship can be seen by considering the practice that is followed in regard to a tug towing a large seagoing barge. It is a common—and very successful—practice to tow a light barge on a hawser in a narrow canal, or in a crooked river. However in such waterways, when the barge is loaded, the tug will be lashed up on the quarter.

10. Lashing Up a Tug to Meet Different Conditions

Different conditions will require that the tug be lashed up differently. If the tug is to be lashed up to something small and easy to handle, and with which she will make considerable headway, then the tug's bow must be well in to prevent the speed from causing the tow to break adrift.

Whenever a tug lashes up to a large ship it will almost certainly be not for the purpose of making speed, but to exert the greatest possible control over the ship. (If a ship is wild enough to need to have a tug lashed up alongside, to keep her under control, she will need at least one more tug to assist her in maneuvering; this tug will, under almost all conditions, serve best on a hawser.)

Suppose we lash the tug up on the ship's starboard quarter—which is, for the greatest number of conditions, the proper side. (See Figure 25.) In "making up" or lashing up the tug, the intention will be to have her in position to act as follows: First, if the ship sheers to starboard the tug's left rudder can be used most effectively in breaking the sheer. Second, if the ship sheers to port the tug can most effectively break the sheer by backing. Fortunately, in this case, when one purpose is best accomplished, the other is accomplished equally well.

Under these circumstances, the proper way to lash up the tug is parallel, or very nearly parallel, with the ship. To illustrate

Figure 25. Tugs lashed up to, and under way with, their tows in a narrow channel.

This schooner, the Ella Pierce Thurlow of Boston, was one of the last sailing vessels to pass through the Sabine-Neches Canal; and on this trip was being piloted by the author.

why this is proper, consider what happens if the tug is not lashed up in this manner but instead her bow is gotten quite a bit in toward the ship's side. If this is the case, then the tug will carry considerable left rudder—for example, say it takes 10 degrees— just to keep the ship steady. Then in the event the ship takes a rank sheer to starboard which could just barely be controlled

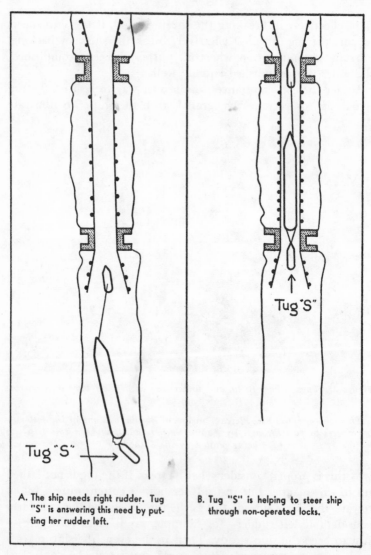

A. The ship needs right rudder. Tug "S" is answering this need by putting her rudder left.

B. Tug "S" is helping to steer ship through non-operated locks.

Figure 26

with full left rudder (if the tug were lashed up parallel with the ship), the tug will be unable to break the sheer because—lashed up with her bow in—the effect of full left or 35 degrees of rudder will be no more than 25 degrees would be if the tug were lashed up parallel.

Also in backing to break a sheer to port, if the tug's bow is in, it means her stern is out. The more the tug's stern is away from the ship when she backs, the greater is the tendency of the tug's backing to pull the ship's stern to starboard, and this in turn causes the ship's bow to go to port—the very thing that the tug is trying to prevent.

By lashing the tug up parallel—when in a narrow canal—another advantage is achieved. Less of the width of the canal is taken up, not only because the tug's stern does not project; but also because the tug causes her tow to go straight ahead instead of obliquely as when the tug's bow is in toward the ship's side.

11. Tug Towed Astern

If a ship "bad" enough to need a tug lashed up on the quarter to steer her is coming to a portion of a waterway too narrow to allow the tug to remain alongside, then the only way a tug can help with the steering is by being towed close astern with a line leading from each quarter of the ship to the tug's bow. If the ship needs the help of right rudder, the tug renders this help by putting her rudder *left*, and vice versa. (See Figure 26, a and b.)

Under any conditions, this is a rather dangerous place for a tug; and it is particularly dangerous with a strong fair tide.

12. Docking with a Slight Fair Tide

In narrow channels—because of limited widths—it is often necessary to turn a ship around while she is light, consequently she might have to be docked *with* the tide instead of head to it.

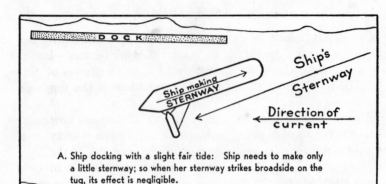

A. Ship docking with a slight fair tide: Ship needs to make only a little sternway; so when her sternway strikes broadside on the tug, its effect is negligible.

B. Ship attempting to dock with a strong fair tide: Ship's excessive sternway will strike broadside on tug and deflect ship's bow to starboard, in spite of the tug backing full speed.

C. Ship docking with a strong fair tide: Tug acts as a rudder and draws ship's bow to port.

Figure 27

Then as an additional adverse factor, tugs might not be easily available. When such is the case, one tug will have to perform the services that normally would call for two or three. The use of only one tug will be described in the following situations.

First let us dock the ship, starboard side to, with only a slight fair tide; wind negligible. The tug will be made fast the same as accounted for in Section 3 of this chapter.

The ship will be turned around well above the dock. As she comes down with the current she will be stopped, a little before arriving abreast of her berth, and placed in a position slightly diagonal to the current, (this will put the current on her port quarter[2]) with her stern toward the dock. (See Figure 27, a.) By gathering only a slight amount of sternway, the ship will quit advancing over the bottom (that is, she will stay abreast of the same portion of the dock).

The tug can—and will—be allowed to swing out at right angles to the ship; and by backing, or "filling" (going ahead), or remaining stopped, the tug can steer the ship, stern first, alongside the dock.

13. DOCKING WITH A VERY STRONG FAIR TIDE

However, an attempt to dock the ship according to the foregoing procedure would most likely be a failure if all the conditions described in the previous section were the same except that there was a *very strong* fair tide. Because with the tug lying on the bow, at right angles to the ship, which would, in this case, necessarily have to gather considerable sternway, the results would quite likely be opposite to those when there is only a little current. To be more explicit:

By backing, the tug should—and ordinarily would—pull the

---

[2] How the tug will cause the ship to get in the desired position can be gathered from the last two paragraphs of Section 4 of this chapter.

ship's bow toward her; however, *excessive* sternway will (when the tug is lying at right angles) cause the tug to act as a drag and will deflect the ship's bow *away* from the tug more than the tug's backing can pull the bow *toward* the tug. Therefore, the ship's bow will be forced *toward* the dock—in spite of the tug's backing—and this in turn will throw the ship's stern *away* from the dock. Then, too, the tug's position will be harmful to the ship in another way. The tug lying broadside to the ship's sternway—by acting as a drag—will make it harder for the ship to gather enough sternway to hold herself against the current. (See Figure 27, b.)

Therefore, when a ship must be docked *with* a *very strong* fair tide, the tug's stern should be held close, but not flat, alongside the ship.[3] When the tug is in this position (*i.e.,* with her stern out just a little from the ship's side) her effect on the ship is just opposite—in two respects—to what it is when she is at right angles. First, the ship's sternway causes the tug (when her stern is out only a little from the ship's side) to act as a rudder and consequently pull the ship's bow toward the tug, and this in turn sets the ship's stern toward the dock. Second, the tug is so near to being parallel with the ship that the tug's backing helps the ship to gather sternway and thereby be better able to hold herself against the current. (See Figure 27, c.)

Then too, in this position the tug is safe, and her lines can be held, regardless of how much sternway the ship may gather, because the tug will be nearly "stern to" the force of the ship's sternway. Whereas, when the ship gets excessive sternway, the tug, if she is at right angles to the ship, is not only in a position that makes it extremely difficult for her lines to be held, but also in a very dangerous position, because she is *broadside* to the ship's sternway.

[3] If the tug were flat alongside, *i.e.,* parallel with the ship, she could help in gathering sternway; however, this position would cause the help in deflecting the ship's bow toward the tug to be inconsequential.

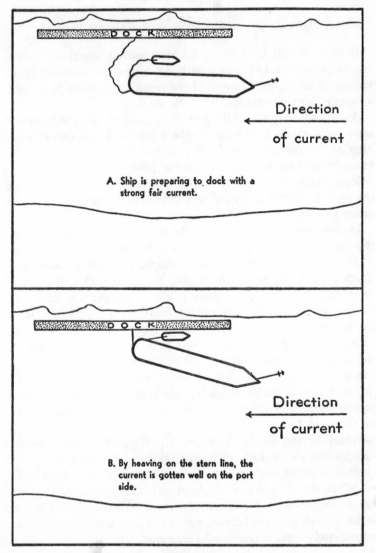

A. Ship is preparing to dock with a strong fair current.

Direction of current

B. By heaving on the stern line, the current is gotten well on the port side.

Direction of current

Figure 28

14. Docking with the Current in a Heavy Freshet

If there should be a heavy freshet running, about the surest and safest way to dock a ship with the current is as follows (providing, of course that abreast of the berth the channel is at least a little wider than the length of the ship):

Anchor the ship about 150 feet off of the dock, so as to have her stern approximately abreast of where her stern line will belong, after she is turned around. (See Figure 28, a.) Put out barely enough chain to enable the anchor to hold.

Run a stern line from the offshore quarter to the location on the dock where the stern line will belong after the ship is turned around.

Let the tug come in between the ship and the dock—head to the current—and take a line from the ship's inshore quarter.

The officer doing the handling should then go aft, since too much time would be lost in passing the word back and forth if he stayed on the bridge. If there is a steering gear and telegraph on the poop it will be very helpful; however, if there is not, then the rudder orders, and the signals to the engine room—and the orders to the forecastlehead—will have to be relayed through the bridge. The man doing the handling must be aft where he can see for himself (1) that the stern is kept clear of the dock; (2) that the tug keeps in the proper position, and pulls at the proper speed; and (3) that just the right amount of strain is kept on the stern line.

When the tug has her line and is pulling, then heave on the line leading to the dock until the heaving causes the force of the current to strike well on the ship's inshore side. (See Figure 28, b.) When the stern is in enough, avast heaving but keep the line on the nigger-head. Now, quickly heave on the anchor until it is just well clear of the bottom; and when it is clear of the bottom, immediately make it ready to let go again.

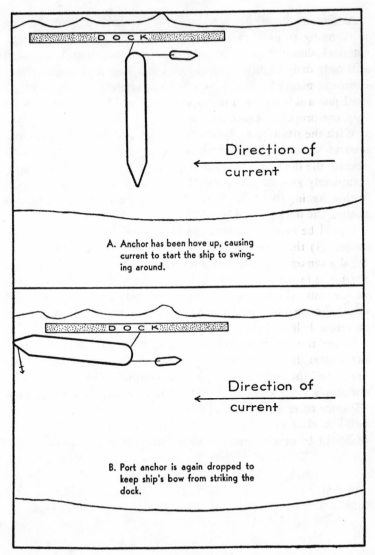

A. Anchor has been hove up, causing current to start the ship to swinging around.

B. Port anchor is again dropped to keep ship's bow from striking the dock.

Figure 29

As soon as the anchor is aweigh, the current will start the ship to swinging around. (See Figure 29, a.) The tug and the line on the dock should be able to hold the stern—or at most, the stern will only drift slightly with the current. The stern line, since it is on the nigger-head, can—by heaving or slacking—be made to hold just a safe strain. The ship's engine will be used to keep the ship the proper distance off the dock.

With the stern being held, the current will make the ship spin around so rapidly that there is danger she might slap heavily against the dock. To prevent this, just a little before the ship is completely around (or parallel with the dock), let go the port anchor again, and hold it just before the bow is about to take against the dock. (See Figure 29, b.)

It will be easy to prevent the bow from striking the dock because: (1) the forward part of the ship (having, especially, in mind a tanker drawing only a few feet forward) causes only slight resistance in the water, and is therefore very easy to check against the current; (2) just before the bow is ready to take (against the dock) the current will have gotten on the inshore side and will therefore help to hold it out.

When the ship gets stern to the current, (1) she already has out a stern line, with a strain on it; (2) the tug is holding her "stern to" the current—and is in a position where she can pull the ship's stern away from the dock, if it should be necessary; (3) since there are no slack lines hanging over the stern, the propeller is clear so it can be used as might be needed. Therefore, it should be easy to land the ship alongside of the dock.

Chapter Six

Use of Anchors to Maneuver

In the summer of 1942 while a single screw ship was under way in the Panama Canal, it was discovered that something was wrong with the steering gear. By skillful use of an anchor, along with the engine, the ship was kept under control until she could be brought to a stop. The incident caused a search for material on the subject of steering ships with anchors, and the Captain of the Port at Balboa distributed copies of the author's article which appeared in the March 1942 issue of the *U. S. Naval Institute Proceedings,* under the title of "The Use of Anchors in Maneuvering." The author is grateful to *U. S. Naval Institute Proceedings* for permission to reprint the article here.

In its early days the Port Arthur Ship Canal was extremely narrow and shallow, and in those days the maneuverability of ships in general was much inferior to what it is today. The result was that vessels very often—to quote the then commonly used expression—"acted as though they had no rudder at all." It was a very frequent occurrence for bad handling ships, especially when loaded, to sheer from bank to bank, and even the best handling ships could be kept steady only when directly in the middle of the canal. Therefore according to the old saying that "necessity is the mother of invention," from "necessity" the use of anchors was resorted to for the sake of keeping ships under control—especially when meeting one another in a narrow channel.

The passing of sailing ships has made the expert handling of them almost a "lost art." Likewise the deepening and widening of inland waterways that are used by ocean vessels has made the use of anchors less of a necessity. However in narrow waterways, where the bottom is soft mud and free from obstructions, the expert use of anchors will always be a valuable aid in maneuvering and it would indeed be a great misfortune to shipping if it became a "lost art."

It is my opinion—gained both from observation and experience—that anchors have on innumerable occasions made it possible to handle ships safely when they otherwise would have met with very serious accidents. I will therefore discuss the following situations:

> When one vessel is about to meet another vessel in a narrow channel (Situations 1, 3, & 9).
> To drop an achor for the purpose of breaking a sheer (Situation 2).
> Ships "smelling the banks" (Situations 3 & 5B).
> To get a ship safely anchored when she has a strong fair tide (Situation 4).
> After a ship has been "jacked" on her anchor, to get under way again (Situation 5).
> The use of an anchor in making turns (Situation 6).
> A tug towing a ship stern first (Situation 7).
> Ways an anchor can be helpful in docking (Situation 8).
> When the channel is obstructed (Situation 10).
> A ship can be kept afloat with a minimum amount of headway (Situation 10B).

SITUATION 1. VESSELS MEETING IN NARROW CHANNELS

It is always considered a serious undertaking, when a ship has headway, to drop an anchor; pay out a scope of chain; and then hold it, intending to drag it along the bottom. *When one vessel is about to meet another vessel in a narrow channel,* and this is advocated, it is considered so hazardous that shipmasters—who are unfamiliar with such a procedure—are invariably reluctant to consent to having it done. Their reluctance is well grounded; because, if the officer on the forecastlehead does not do just exactly right, a serious mishap—caused by the anchor holding instead of dragging on the bottom—is likely to ensue. Nevertheless, if the anchor is dropped just right, the chance of a mishap is so slight that it is entirely offset by the almost absolutely perfect control that a ship can be put under contrasted with the possibility of her otherwise being almost, if not completely, out of control. How to accomplish these desired results will be subsequently covered.

SITUATION 2. DROPPING ANCHOR TO BREAK A SHEER

No doubt almost all pilots and towboat men, whose job it is to handle ships in close quarters with strange crews, have on occasions been seriously handicapped and sometimes made helpless simply because they could not get their orders properly executed, owing to the fact that local conditions required some procedure that was entirely unfamiliar to the crew; and furthermore, if the facts could be known, men handling ships under such conditions no doubt have deliberately allowed accidents to happen for fear of having more serious ones simply because they felt certain they could not get their orders properly executed. Probably in no better way could this state of affairs be illustrated than in the need *to drop an anchor for the purpose of breaking a sheer* in order to avoid a collision with a ship that is being met. It should be done as follows:

(*a*) If possible have the bar in the brake wheel. When the order is given to let go, release the brake sufficiently to allow the chain to run freely over the wildcat. The anchor will hit the bottom so suddenly that several fathoms of slack will come in the chain and it will then, of its own accord, for a few moments stop paying out. At this instant the brake must be set up not just hand tight—but as tight as possible with the use of the brake bar and not just the weight of one man on the bar but an extra man or two. Believe it or not (to use Ripley's expression) even though the ship has considerable headway, the brake can be securely set before the chain gets a heavy strain on it. Then when the strain does come the anchor, instead of holding, is jerked out of the mud and because the chain is so near up and down, the anchor will drag along the bottom without getting a good hold.

(*b*) Now, when a ship is just starting to take a sheer, if the anchor is dropped and given just this short scope of chain, it will almost invariably break the sheer. And even though it doesn't it will retard the sheer sufficiently to allow the other vessel time to get safely past.

(*c*) The thought that is now apt to be in the reader's mind is: Why not go full speed astern? The answer is: with a right-handed single screw ship sheering away from her own starboard hand bank—if backed —at first will almost certainly act as though she has a left-handed propeller; furthermore, during the time the propeller is motionless, while the engine is being put in astern motion, the effectiveness of the rudder is almost entirely lost thereby causing the sheer to greatly increase. Even with an outboard turning twin screw ship when she takes a sheer away from the bank and the propeller nearest the bank is backed the effect, at least at first, quite often is to increase the sheer instead of breaking it.

(*d*) An anchor should be used in the above manner if a ship unexpectedly takes a sheer when she is so close to the vessel she is meeting that there is not time to take any further action.

Situation 3. Passing an Approaching Vessel

Next let us suppose the *Ship*—while she has the channel to herself—is *"smelling the banks"* to such an extent that it is quite evident she cannot be held on her side in passing an approaching vessel.

(*a*) First, of course, reduce the speed as much as possible. Then drop the anchor[1] in the above described manner.[2] Drag the anchor over the bottom for some distance. This should be done for several reasons. The flukes, after a while, get balled up with mud which keeps them from getting too much of a hold on the bottom. After this has occurred the chain can be slacked out and then held—but only with reasonable certainty—if it is properly done. The proper procedure is to slack only from a few links to about a fathom and set not just hand tight but, again, as tight as two or three men can do with the bar. This action always causes one and generally causes two things to happen. It is certain that the friction on the brake band, when the chain is stopped, always causes it to get at least slightly hot. And it generally happens that the sudden jerk on the anchor causes the balled up mud on the flukes to come off with the result that it takes a firmer grip on the bottom. After being dragged along, the flukes will generally again become packed with mud and thereby ease the strain on the chain; and in the meantime the brake band will get cooled off and thereby lessen the danger of its not holding. Two questions are now probably running through the reader's mind.

(*b*) First, why not stop the ship if she is steering so poorly? The answer is: If a loaded ship is behaving so badly it takes a long time, and even then it is extremely difficult, to get her completely stopped except by using an anchor. If the anchor is not used in stopping her there is a strong likelihood of her striking the bank or getting "jacked" (crosswise in the channel). And in the case of a light ship with a strong beam wind she will most surely blow against the bank and will then probably not be able to get under way again.

(*c*) Second, the reader is apt to wonder how it can be known what the condition of the anchor is while it is on the bottom. Of course, there is no way to tell absolutely what the condition of the anchor is but "mud pilots" do know that sometimes when dragging an anchor with, say, 15 fathoms of chain, it will hold well for a while and then all of a sudden will give the impression that the anchor has become unshackled. It

[1] Sit. 4*d*.
[2] Sit. 2*a*.

sometimes happens, when this occurs, that 30 or more fathoms of chain can be paid out without having as much effect as the 15 fathoms originally had.

(*d*) Another thing to substantiate the opinion that the flukes become balled up with mud is that, after the anchor has been dragged, when it is hove up it is almost always in that condition.

(*e*) With a little time and patience sufficient chain can be paid out to kill the ship's headway—if it is deemed necessary—even with the engine working ahead slow at intervals or continuously. If enough chain has been paid out to prevent the ship from ranging ahead with the engine working slow, then if it is desired to make her gather headway it can be done by working full ahead. Under these circumstances even an extremely bad handling ship improves to the extent that she is under practically as effective control as an automobile on a paved street, because she can be held in almost any position for an indefinite length of time, can be made to answer her helm without gathering headway, and can be stopped by simply stopping the engine; and almost, if not exactly, the instant the engine is put in reverse motion the ship starts gathering sternway.

Situation 4. Anchoring with a Strong Fair Tide

(*a*) Let us now consider the most difficult as well as the most dangerous thing to do. It is: *To get a ship safely anchored when she has a strong fair tide* and is in a channel that is too narrow for her to swing around in, and where the banks are so nearly straight up and down that a vessel can land and lie against them somewhat similar to lying against a dock.

(*b*) To make the illustration clear, assume that the ship has a right-handed propeller and is in a straight reach of a canal. First get the ship almost but not quite dead in the water and also have her not in the middle but as near the starboard hand bank as is possible without her wanting, too much, to run away from it. (The slower she goes the nearer she can be held to the bank.) When this has been accomplished and she is steady and parallel with the bank drop the port anchor in the manner previously described.[3] In spite of the fact that the intention is to bring the ship to anchor, paradoxically, the anchor must not hold on the bottom but must drag.

(*c*) It has just been stated that the ship should be almost but not quite

[3] Sit. 2*a* & 3*a*.

dead in the water when the anchor is dropped. The reason for this is: if the ship does not have a little headway when the anchor takes the bottom it is difficult to keep her "stern to" to the current. However, she must be kept in this position which also means (in this particular case) parallel to the bank. Little by little, slack on the chain till there is out about 15 fathoms in the water (the exact scope being the very least that will have the required effect). By the time this has been accomplished the ship should still be close to the starboard bank (but if not she must be maneuvered into that position) and probably will be ranging ahead over the bottom but making a little sternway in the water. By this time the anchor will probably have balled up with mud so as not to hold too much and the ship can be "felt out" to see just how she will act.

(*d*) If time will permit—the safest way to get the anchor down is to heave it out; after it is on the bottom, then in heaving out chain be governed by the aforesaid comments.[4] And of course keep the brake set when the anchor is not being hove.

(*e*) Holding a ship "stern to" to the current with the anchor down is somewhat similar to the manner in which a man keeps the end of a pole balanced in the palm of his hand. He must move his hand one way and then the other to offset the effect of gravity. The anchor acts on the ship in the same manner, to the extent that it holds her bow—which corresponds to the lower end of the pole—but since the anchor can't be moved about to offset the effect of the current (which is the same to the ship as gravity is to the pole) being first on one side and then on the other—this is accomplished by the use of the propeller and rudder.

(*f*) With the necessary amount of chain out the ship is ready to be put to anchor. Give her a kick ahead on a full left rudder. Stop her when she answers. She will now have the current on the port quarter which will set her stern towards the bank. If judgment has been accurate a number of things will have been accomplished. The ship will be almost—but not quite—parallel to the bank, she will have lost her headway over the bottom, the strain on the chain will be eased and she will be setting bodily towards the bank, and will fetch up against it with her starboard quarter. The quarter will have a tendency to stick to the bank which will make it possible for the ship to be held by the anchor in spite of the fact that it is probably balled up with mud and there is only a little chain out.

(*g*) To account for the ship being put against the starboard bank and the port anchor being used: I will ask that the reader visualize how after the ship was given a kick ahead on a left rudder—to get the cur-

[4] Sit. 2a & 3a.

rent on the port side—the leverage caused by the bow being retarded would cause the stern to swing heavily towards the bank. Now the tendency to back to port will help to make it possible for the ship to land gently. After she has landed she will lie there when more nearly parallel (which—with reference to the rudder, propeller, etc.—is the safest position) with the port chain leading astern on the port side.

(*h*) Of course a great deal of this maneuvering can be done away with in "jacking" (as anchoring a ship in this position is called) but only by greatly increasing the likelihood of doing damage to the most delicate as well as the most essential, exposed part of the hull, i.e., the stern frame, rudder, and propeller.

Situation 5. Getting a "Jacked" Ship Under Way Again

We will now assume that *after the ship has been "jacked" on her anchor* we want *to get under way again.* Maybe it will be an easy job. A number of things have been done to make it so. Let us recount and comment on them.

(*a*) First, with the ship alongside the starboard bank, there will be a clear lead on the port chain whereas the starboard chain and anchor would lead under the ship.

(*b*) Next, the very least possible scope of chain was let out in hopes of being able to heave it home. If it can be hove home, after that has been done, it might seem that there was nothing to do but "hook her up" and go ahead. Instead caution should be used in getting the ship away from the bank and into the middle of the canal. She should be worked ahead (and under almost all circumstances just slow). In all probability her head will swing to port even though the rudder is put full right; if she does this having been anchored on the starboard bank is a big asset, because after her bow has headed out till it is about in the middle of the canal, by backing a little—before she has gathered enough headway to cause her to "smell the bank" too much—she should back to port and throw her stern towards the middle of the canal. Since her bow has gotten out there already, simply come ahead and steady her up.

(*c*) Now suppose the anchor can't be hove home. With the ship practically parallel to the bank, when she is backed the suction from the bank on the starboard quarter should just about offset the pitch of the wheel and cause her to back straight, thereby getting the chain up and down so the anchor can be hove home.

(*d*) But suppose the anchor can't be hove up and she won't go astern (two quite common conditions). Here is where the importance of having a short scope of chain comes in. The anchor can be dragged [5] by working the ship ahead until she can be maneuvered into the middle of the canal. Then by skillful handling she can be backed straight astern sufficiently to get the anchor up. The port anchor leading astern on the port side makes it much easier to back a right-handed ship straight than would be the case if it were the starboard anchor leading astern on the starboard side.

SITUATION 6. USE OF ANCHOR IN MAKING TURNS

Next will be taken up *the use of an anchor in making turns* that are so sharp they cannot be made by simply putting the rudder hard over.

I will refer to a particular section of the waterway where I am a pilot and tell what was, before the channel was widened and deepened, the only way the swing could be made with a deep loaded ship.

(*a*) Think of the capital letter *L* upside down and you have a mental picture of the waterway at this point. All along the base of the *L* is a dock. It might be well to emphasize that this is a right-angle turn and furthermore that it is on a left rudder which makes it the most difficult for a right-handed single screw ship.

Before approaching this turn the port anchor will be dropped and little by little given chain till the scope that has been paid out is sufficient to almost stop the ship's headway with the engine working slow ahead. This will generally be somewhere between 15 and 30 fathoms. The anchor must be dropped soon enough to get the necessary amount of chain out and have the ship all but stopped just before she is at the point where the swing must be made. If in handling the ship it has been found that she is unusually sluggish on her rudder then at this particular time stop the engine and at the same instant slack out 2 or 3 fathoms of chain. When she brings up on the chain it will snub her and stop her. Now go slow ahead and in the meantime the rudder will have been put full left. The anchor chain is now being used in about the same fashion as a spring line is used in bringing a ship around the corner of a dock and into a slip.

SITUATION 7. USE OF ANCHOR WHEN TUG IS TOWING SHIP STERN FIRST

The next situation is that of *a tug towing a ship stern first;* and because it requires the most precise use of anchors, consider the ship to be

[5] Sit. 3*e*.

a light single screw tanker, about 500 feet in length, drawing roughly 3 feet forward and 16 feet aft. Have a strong beam wind blowing. Let the tide be slack. Imagine the waterway to be about 400 feet in width and the distance the ship has to be towed astern to be approximately 2,000 feet. The ship has the use of her main engine.

(*a*) In getting ready to start the ship astern the tug will first be given a stern line and will—heading in the opposite direction to the ship—commence pulling. The weather anchor will be dropped as far to windward as possible. Now here is a case in which you want the anchor to hold, and you don't want it to hold, both at the same time. And it can almost be made to do just that.

(*b*) It is desired that the anchor should keep the ship from drifting to leeward but at the same time allow her to go astern. In this instance it would be entirely wrong to drop the anchor just to the bottom and let it drag. Instead, when it is dropped it is necessary that a sufficient scope of chain be paid right out so that when it comes tight it will prevent the ship from going to leeward. This will be about 30 fathoms on the wildcat. If the anchor holds and the tug pulls astern, and to windward as much as possible, in a little while the chain will be leading almost directly ahead. Let us presume when the chain leads thus and has a strain on it, that the tug's power alone will not be sufficient to make the anchor drag.

(*c*) Right here is a good place to explain the knack of making the anchor drag astern but not drag to leeward. As has just been stated, the first requirement is that there be sufficient chain out to keep the wind alone from making her drag the anchor. The other secret is to go very slowly. In dragging our tanker astern we will keep these two things in mind.

(*d*) Now the position of the tug is just a trifle to windward of directly astern and she is pulling full speed. The anchor chain is leading a trifle to windward of directly ahead and has a heavy strain on it. The ship is lying motionless. In order to make her start astern we signal slow astern on the engine. The engine works astern but no results. So we go half astern. Still no results. The anchor must have a good hold. So full speed astern. The ship starts gathering sternway so we change the engine to slow astern; however her sternway increases instead of lessening and we also regret to note that her bow is going rapidly to leeward. We stop the engine and immediately slack the chain till there is 30 fathoms in the water. This stops her bow from falling off but when the chain leads ahead again—then the tug is unable to pull the ship astern. So slow astern on the ship's engine. This time slow astern gets the same results that full astern did the previous time.[6] The engine is stopped. But the ship is not only still going astern but her bow is going to leeward, so the chain is paid out till there is 45 fathoms on the windlass. This stops her from going to leeward but also from going astern. Slow astern on the engine. No results. Half astern. Now she gathers a little sternway, but also her bow goes to leeward. Stop her again. She soon becomes dead in the water. It is not advisable to pay out much, if any, more chain because if the anchor should get well settled on the bottom it could not be dragged any more. Therefore drop the other, or lee, anchor on the bottom and let it have only a fathom or two of slack chain. This second anchor so used is surprisingly effective in preventing the bow from going to leeward but has a neglible effect in retarding the ship's sternway. Now go astern on the engine at whatever speed necessary to make the ship get sternway but be quick to stop whenever she gathers speed.

(*e*) By maneuvering in the above manner a ship can almost always be towed the necessary distance astern before her bow gets too far down to leeward, and if she does drift into something it will be so gently that no damage should be done.

SITUATION 8. USE OF ANCHOR IN DOCKING

Let us consider some of the *ways an anchor can be helpful in docking:*

(*a*) In the first hypothetical case we will make a starboard side landing with a single screw right-handed ship, loaded so deep she is "smelling the bottom" and therefore taking a lot of rudder to make her answer with the engine working slow ahead. She will not answer at all with the engine stopped. While still a good distance from the dock drop the port anchor and little by little give her almost enough chain to stop her with the engine working slow ahead. This will entirely eliminate the likelihood of having too much headway when getting close to the dock and also avoid the danger of hitting the dock when, and if,[7] she is backed for the purpose of stopping.

(*b*) The reader is quite likely to be thinking: The anchor is apt to damage or go through the ship's bottom. Although this could happen, it is a remote probability if the bottom is soft mud and (it might be well to emphasize) if the anchor is dropped in the aforesaid manner,[8] because: (1) the anchor buries itself in the mud; (2) the flukes and crown

[6] Sit. 3*c* & 3*d*.
[7] Sit. 3*e*.
[8] Sit. 2*a* & 4*d*.

become balled up with mud; (3) the shank and flukes will not point in the direction which would be necessary to cause them to penetrate. However the anchor can and very often does do serious damage if—when it is dropped—a great deal of chain is paid right out. There are two distinct reasons: (1) By giving too much slack the chain can get foul of the flukes and thereby prevent the anchor from leading properly when it starts to drag. (2) If given too much chain the anchor—when it strikes—might lie on the bottom with the crown farthest ahead thus making the shank and shackle point aft. In either of these instances, when the strain does come on the chain, the result will be about the same as when a fishhook is backed out of the flesh.

Dropping an anchor is considered so extremely simple that very little if any thought is ever given to doing it properly. Therefore when a mishap occurs it is thought of as being unavoidable, whereas in many cases damage could have been prevented if the anchor had been handled properly.

(c) In the next hypothetical case let us go to the other extreme and assume we have a ship in ballast or (to use the coined expression) "flying light," with a very strong beam wind blowing on the dock. The dock is parallel to the channel, slack tide. In plenty of time before nearing the dock drop the lee anchor and little by little "feel" her out till satisfied she has ample chain.

(d) It might be well to go into detail as to what is "ample chain." The stronger the wind, the more the chain has to be paid out; and incidentally the stronger the engine must be worked. The ultimate purpose is to have the anchor hold the bow up against the wind, and lee rudder hold the stern sufficiently up to windward. Under this kind of control a ship can be barely making headway and still make practically no leeway. The ship is now in such shape that she can be worked right up alongside the dock slow enough to get lines out, both fore and aft, before ever stopping the propeller.

(e) Now let us consider the same ship landing at the same dock under the same conditions, except that the wind is blowing heavy off the dock. The same procedure would be carried out. Of course the opposite anchor would be the lee anchor.

(f) Those who are unfamiliar with this maneuver almost invariably contend that, in both of the above cases, the weather anchor would be more effective in holding the bow up to windward, and conversely that the lee anchor would cause its chain to act as a spring line and consequently pull her head down to leeward.

(g) Ordinarily these viewpoints are correct, therefore let us try to find out what causes these improbabilities. But first this illustration or comparison: A doctor avoids as much as possible the use of narcotics because he is ever mindful that they can and sometimes do have disastrous consequences. Therefore one of the secrets of their successful use is that they be administered as sparingly as possible. Likewise a "mud pilot" is ever mindful of the serious difficulties that can be caused by dropping an anchor and not being able to hold it, so he avoids its use whenever possible; and one of the secrets of its successful use is that always the minimum scope of chain, to get the desired results, be paid out.

(h) It might be well to repeat that we are considering a light ship with a strong beam wind. Now before either anchor would be dropped the ship's headway should be reduced to the minimum. This reduced speed will cause her to go to leeward almost as much as she goes ahead. Under these circumstances if the lee anchor is dropped it will not lead from the hawse pipe but from under the bottom of the ship, and toward the weather side. Therefore, with a very little chain, the anchor will have a great deal of effect, because leading from under the ship will make it more parallel with the bottom and therefore have a decided tendency to help anchor dig into the mud and hold better.

(i) On the other hand if the weather anchor is dropped, the chain leads directly from the hawse pipe which necessitates considerable chain to keep the effect on the anchor from being just "up and down."

(j) The lee anchor will hold with much less pressure on the brake band—under the above conditions—because the bight of the chain pressing so heavily against the side of the ship helps it to be held for the same reason that taking an extra turn on the bitts helps a line to hold.

(k) If it were desired simply to hold the bow up then the weather anchor would, in most if not all cases, be preferable. But the anchor is used not only to hold the bow but to help hold the entire ship broadside to the wind. When a ship is in this situation the major concern is to see that the rudder is able to hold her stern up to windward. Of course the most effective way to accomplish this is to go full speed ahead with full lee rudder. In the event the anchor only drags slightly—and incidentally that is what we want it to do—there is danger that full ahead on a full lee rudder will not work the stern up, so it is of utmost importance that full use has been made of everything else at our command. In this particular case that thing is the lee anchor. Let us see what it now does. (Keep in mind that the anchor is leading under the bottom and to windward.) When the ship is worked full ahead it causes her to go up to windward till the chain leads aft along the lee side. When this takes place the chain ceases to serve as a breast line and becomes (according to those who would question its use instead of the weather anchor) a spring line leading from the lee bow and is exceedingly effective in helping the rudder to twist (or swing) the after part of the ship up to windward.

(*l*) Now think—in contrast—what the weather anchor would do. It would act as a spring leading from the weather bow and would cause results exactly opposite to what we desperately need. It would help the wind to throw the stern still more to leeward.

Situation 9. Meeting and Passing in a Narrow Channel

Let us now revert to *ships meeting and passing one another*. A light ship making so much leeway—because of a strong beam wind—as to make it unsafe to meet and pass an approaching ship, can eliminate practically all danger by using the anchor as heretofore described.[9]

Situation 10. Preventing Light Ship from Grounding

The last situation exists *when the channel is obstructed* at a point some distance ahead and it is necessary to stop a light ship that is encountering a strong beam wind; and in stopping the ship still keep her afloat, or off the bank.

(*a*) A light ship with a strong beam wind in a narrow waterway is under conditions a great deal similar to those that confront an airplane in the air. As long as the airplane can keep sufficient headway she can stay aloft. When she loses headway she falls to the ground. As long as a light ship can keep headway she can keep from grounding. Let her lose headway and she falls against the bank.

(*b*) But to contradict myself: *A light ship* encountering a strong beam wind in a narrow waterway can under many conditions be kept afloat without making headway. When conditions such as a fair tide or an extremely strong beam wind make it impossible to completely stop, she *can be kept afloat with a minimum amount of headway*. This can be accomplished in a manner previously described.[10]

[9] Sit. 2*a* & 3*a*.
[10] Sit. 2*a*, 3*a*, 3*e*, 4*d*, 4*e*, 8*c*, 8*d*, 8*h*, 8*i*, 8*j*, 8*k*, 8*l*.

From one viewpoint, revealing these secrets could have the effect of giving away one's patent rights. However, I take the view that if these facts are thoroughly understood by all deck officers it will make my job much easier as well as help me to avoid accidents.

As a speaker or actor can "feel" the reaction he is causing on his audience; likewise the pilot can "feel" the reaction on the ship's officers that is caused by the way he is handling the ship. And there is nothing that makes a pilot's job quite so difficult and disheartening as to know that he is doing the right thing and not have the officers' co-operation and sympathy because they think he is doing things that are unnecessary or wrong.

Therefore, the goal of this article is to bring about a better understanding between ships' officers and pilots, and thereby cause ships to be more efficiently handled.

Conclusion

Whenever the capabilities of a ship vastly exceed the strength of the wind, current and suction, then "muddling through" will succeed. In such cases a ship can be "bulldozed" through many maneuvers.

But, whenever a ship's capability is closely balanced by the elements, then bulldozing will often fail at times when techniques recommended in the text will bring about a successful maneuver.

Since, in practice, the strength of the natural elements cannot be exactly judged, the prudent shiphandler will assume these adversaries to be stronger than they probably are.

By adhering to this practice some "unavoidable" accidents might be avoided.

Appendix

1. Minimizing Suction with a Twin-Screw Ship

Except for an element whose effect will be discussed in the next section, any ship in a narrow canal will steer best when she gets an equal amount of suction on each quarter.

With a single-screw ship always (excepting the element referred to above), and a twin-screw ship sometimes, this means a ship will steer best when in the middle of a canal or narrow channel.

But there are times when a twin-screw ship will be unmanageable if she is handled in a conventional manner, i.e., with both propellers turning at the same speed. This is accounted for by the axiom: the slower a ship goes, the less suction she creates. Therefore, when a twin-screw ship's speed must be less than the speed she will make with both engines working ahead slow, she can, in many instances, be kept under control in this manner: leave one engine—say the starboard—stopped, and work the other ahead slow.

This "lopsided" procedure creates several situations. First, with the starboard engine stopped, the suction that would be created by the starboard propeller is eliminated. Second, the ship will be strongly inclined to go to starboard because the suction created by the port propeller does not have suction (normally created by the starboard propeller) to counteract it. Even if in open water where there is no bank suction and with only the port propeller working, the ship will be inclined to go to starboard.

Therefore, to steer a twin-screw ship with only one propeller working—let's say the port—she must be kept close enough to the starboard bank (bearing in mind the axiom: the nearer the bank, the stronger the suction) in order to receive almost equal suction pull from both banks.

Actually, she must be kept even closer because there is an additional condition that starboard bank suction must counterbalance—the tendency (existing also in open water) for the port propeller to cause the ship to go to starboard.

To elaborate on the foregoing: Headway, on any ship with the propeller stopped, creates some suction; the same amount of headway with the propeller turning creates a greater amount of suction. Furthermore, the propeller of a twin-screw ship creates more suction than that created by a single-screw ship because the twin-screw ship's propeller is nearer the bank.

It should be readily seen that a conventional twin-screw ship (i.e., a twin-screw ship with only one rudder) is much more difficult to steer when in a narrow canal than is a single-screw ship. This is true primarily because the rudder does not get the full force of the wheel-water. To elaborate on the fact that a twin-screw ship's propeller creates more suction, let us suppose the ship gets close enough to the starboard bank that full right rudder together with stopping the starboard engine will not break the sheer. The next thing to do is work the starboard propeller astern. In open water this recourse is almost certain to secure the desired result. However, in a narrow canal the suction created by working the propeller astern is more likely to pull the *stern* toward the starboard bank than the propeller's holding-back effect will pull the *bow* to starboard. In other words, backing one of the propellers of a twin-screw ship for the purpose of breaking a sheer is apt to be futile.

This being the case, why would this method of steering a poorly handling twin-screw ship with a single propeller working be advocated if there is so much likelihood of a sheer developing? To answer, we repeat the axiom: The slower a ship goes, the less suction she creates. A brief summary of some facts follows.

Extremely slow speed together with the negative effect of a stopped propeller creates very little suction. On the other hand —or, on the other side of the ship—the positive effect of the port propeller working ahead together with hard right rudder should overcome the weak amount of suction that will be created by the stopped starboard propeller and very slow speed.

A ship that cannot be handled in the aforesaid manner needs the assistance of a tug (or tugs). How to make best use of a tug in such a case is told in Section 10, page 82. Only the propeller on the side opposite to the tug should be worked, not only because by so doing the ship can be handled best, but even more importantly, because the working of the propeller next to the tug will create suction so powerful that the tug might be broken adrift and sucked into the ship's quarter.

It has been pointed out that headway with the propeller stopped creates less suction than is created with the propeller turning. This being the case, it often happens that a twin-screw ship that cannot be steered with both propellers working ahead slow can be steered with one propeller stopped and the other propeller working ahead half-speed continuously, or at least part of the time.

With one propeller stopped and the other working ahead slow if only a little rudder is required to keep the ship steady, then the speed (on the working propeller) can be increased to half. But be quick to reduce speed as soon as much more rudder is required.

A twin-screw ship that has twin rudders generally steers well in a narrow canal because the full force of the wheel-water strikes the rudders. Should such a ship be "wild" with both engines working (she might be wild because the propellers are nearer the banks) she probably can be kept under perfect (steering) control by working only one propeller. In this situation she should be handled in a manner similar to that which must be resorted to in handling a twin-screw ship that has but one rudder.

2. WIND VERSUS BANK SUCTION

A strong beam wind is the "element" mentioned in the previous section that will cause a light, single-screw ship to steer best in a narrow canal or channel when she receives the greater amount of suction on the lee quarter. Before explaining why, let us see what takes place otherwise.

When an effort is made to keep such a ship in the middle, part of the time she will be a little closer to one bank than she is to the other. It will be practically impossible to keep her perfectly steady. Should she get considerably closer to the windward bank, there is a probability that the increased suction together with the force of the wind will be more effective than hardover rudder. In such a case she will run into the lee bank. This probability may be avoided as follows:

Let the ship's stern drop down to leeward just enough to cause the suction from the lee bank to be counterbalanced by the force of the wind. The outcome will be a desirable one. The ship will be handled in a safer manner, since only a slight amount of rudder—on either side—will be required. In fact, wind and suction often become equally balanced and as long as they remain so, the rudder can be left amidships.

3. ANCHORING IN THE MIDDLE OF A RIVER

There are rivers where cutoffs have eliminated sharp bends. These abandoned portions of a river are used as anchorages in many instances. (See Chart C, page x.)

When a ship is longer than the river's width—and the longer she is, the safer she will be—the ship should be put to anchor in the following manner. With the ship having headway, drop one anchor in the middle. Then, with the ship continuing up the middle, pay out twice the amount of chain that is to be used. When this (double) amount of chain has been paid out, drop the second anchor and stop the ship's headway.

To illustrate, and this would generally be approximately the proper amount, let us say that 60 fathoms of chain have been paid out to the anchor that was dropped first. Now, cause the ship to go astern. The safest way to accomplish this is for a tug to tow the ship astern. As she goes astern, pay out on the chain of the last dropped anchor and at the same time shorten up the chain of the first dropped anchor. When 30 fathoms of the chain have been given to the last dropped anchor, the chain to the first dropped anchor should have been shortened to 30 fathoms. At this instant, hold everything. There should now be a good strain on both chains but in case this is not so, heave in on one chain sufficiently to cause both chains to have a strain.

Many desirable things will have been accomplished: (a) the bow will be held in the middle; (b) with the bow in the middle, if and when the ship falls over to one side or the other (and this is likely to happen), she will be near enough broadside to the direction of the river to cause her quarter—more than the vulnerable rudder and propeller—to rest against the bank; (c) but if these vulnerable parts do get in the mud, it is quite improbable that they will be damaged, providing the ship does not move ahead or astern appreciably; (d) the strain on the chains will prevent the ship from ranging ahead or astern.

Of course, a ship can enter the anchorage (old river) stern-first and be put to anchor in a similar manner. In such a case she will generally need a tug to keep her bow in the middle in addition to the one towing astern.

4. Avoiding Crooked Water When Making a Sharp Bend

In a wide, deep river suction is completely disregarded because its effects are insignificant. In such rivers when there is a slight to moderate downstream current, the customary practice—contrary to the one which must be adhered to in a shallow, narrow river—is to approach the bend from "under the point." By so doing a ship generally receives the benefits of a weaker head current, slack water and a fair current. Furthermore, whenever the strength of the downstream current increases, the benefits will increase proportionally.

With a heavy freshet the last-named "benefit" changes to a serious hazard that should be avoided. (See Chart D, page xiv.) When a ship comes out from under the point her bow will suddenly be struck with much of the force of the downstream current while her stern will still be getting the now harmful effect of the (upstream) countercurrent. The longer a ship, the more vulnerable she becomes to the effects of these conflicting currents.

Therefore, in a heavy freshet, a sharp bend should be approached, not from under the point, but with the ship deep in the bend. By doing this she will completely avoid the hazard of crooked water.

5. When a Tug is Not Available

There are times when a ship must turn around in a narrow channel unassisted. In such a case if the ship is heading upstream and there is, say, an ebb tide and the wind is blowing upstream, it is improbable that the ship can be turned by "backing and filling," particularly if she is light.

When these conditions exist, as a rule, the ship will turn no more than halfway around. Therefore, after getting the ship crosswise of the channel, give her very slight sternway. Then stop the engine and put the rudder *amidships*. The ship will go stern-first into the bank gently and the bow will now drift downstream.

This maneuver sounds hazardous, nevertheless the outcome of backing and filling is far more likely to cause the ship to *unintentionally* be backed into the bank, not gently with the propeller stopped and the rudder amidships, but probably with the propeller in motion and the rudder hard over.

It might be well to comment that if a ship goes stern-first into the bank with the rudder hard over and the propeller in motion, damage is likely to result.

In order for the ship to head downstream, after her stern becomes grounded, the ebb tide must cause more drift than that caused by the wind.

Of course, this maneuver can be resorted to only when the bank is soft mud.

Appendix To
Third Edition

The principal aim of this edition is to explain, more clearly with additional drawings—and a picture—the subjects that have previously been discussed.

Note: The amount of chain to be used is given for ships about 500 feet long with other dimensions in proportion. For larger, and especially much deeper ships the amount of chain that will be required will be proportionately greater.

The theme of this edition can be summarized by the observation that: *If powerful medicines are administered improperly they are apt to do more harm than good.*
Likewise:
If BOW-WAVE, SUCTION and SPEED are ADMINISTERED IMPROPERLY they can cause MORE HARM than good.

Comments & Illustrations
about
Suction, Bow-Wave and Speed
With Sketches of Portions of
The
SABINE DISTRICT WATERWAYS
as they were in 1916

Commentary: When a big ship is in a very narrow and crooked waterway the greater the speed the greater, or the more powerful, is the suction and bow-wave.

Before proceeding with the discussion we will differentiate suction's two meanings. Loosely, it consists of three elements, namely, speed, suction and bow-wave. However, strictly speaking it is the pull, of the water, that is created abreast of a ship's quarters. (In this discussion suction will be referred to with both meanings.)

After having given these variable definitions it again will be stated; THE GREATER THE SPEED THE GREATER, OR THE MORE POWERFUL, IS THE SUCTION AND BOW-WAVE.

With just a little experience this axiom can be adhered to with a reasonable degree of proficiency, providing the channel is not too narrow and crooked and the ship handles good. However, this will not be true if she is a bad handling one. In this case "bad" means a ship that is strongly affected by suction and also is weak on rudder power. With such a ship it is essential to constantly be on guard against the probability that she will take an uncontrollable sheer. It is like a man on a

114

tight rope. He might wobble a little and recover. But if he wobbles too much he will fall. The same thing is true with a ship in a narrow canal. She might "wobble" or sheer a little and recover. But if she sheers too much she will go wild. If and when this happens she will strike the bank; then, most always, glance off; and, without losing much headway, take a run for the opposite side. The reason she will not lose much headway is because the best way to prevent jacking is to keep the engine working ahead. Why this is true will be explained later with illustrations. Also to be explained later is the technique that is required to again get the ship steadied up in the middle of the canal.

With the aforesaid conditions it should be seen a ship needs to be handled in a precise manner.

To emphasize the importance of this assertion baseball pitchers will be used for a parallel. Only the most proficient make the major leagues. Out of this assemblage just a small minority become outstandingly successful. Nevertheless, generally speaking, there is only a slight difference in the capability of the pitcher who retires a batter and the one who allows a home run.

A similar situation confronts the man who is in charge of a big ship when she is in very confined waters. By utilizing headway, suction and bow-wave in just exactly the proper manner his ship is apt to be kept under control. Otherwise, she probably will go wild.

Now will be shown illustrations that pertain to these comments:

A nearly loaded ship drawing 24'-6" has just gotten underway in a river where the controlling channel depth is 25'. Shortly after leaving the dock it was found that she was bad about wanting to run away from shoal water and also weak on rudder power. Therefore the primary precaution was taken. That precaution is to proceed with a minimum amount of headway. Consequently, the engine was worked dead slow.

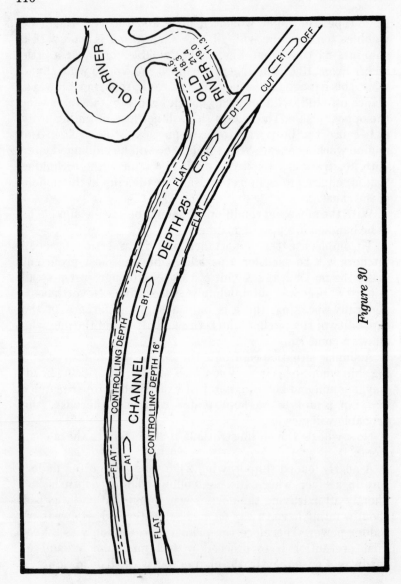

Figure 30

A1. She has just entered the narrow channel that has a gentle bend. Of course the pilot has a mental picture of the channel. Even so, he must resort to having the ship "smell" her way around the bend. In order to accomplish this she is worked up close enough to her port hand side so that even with 5 or 10 degrees of left rudder she swings gently to the right.)

B1. The water has become deeper in the bend with the result that only about 5 degrees of left rudder are needed to sufficiently check the right swing.

C1. The wave pressure on the port bow is suddenly lost. This loss (of wave pressure) calls for easing of the rudder.

D1. By the time the rudder is amidships the suction, on the port quarter, has been lost. To counterbalance this loss of suction required 5 or 10 degrees of right rudder. Then in order to continue the swing sufficiently fast to make the ship head into the middle of the cut still required about the same amount of right rudder to offset the suction on the starboard quarter.

E1. Upon entering the cut there will be a constant pull from suction on both quarters. This pull frequently will require at least 5 or 10 degrees of rudder, first on one side and then on the other, to keep her steady. (If she were going slow -- instead of dead slow -- 10 or 15 degrees would be required.) If, and when she gets slightly closer to either bank, the amount of rudder that will be required to keep her steady will increase rapidly.

NOTE: 1 The statement "the constant pull from suction on both quarters" is apt to give the impression that the ship might sheer rapidly from one side to the other. On the contrary, since she will have a minimum amount of headway, the sheers will be gentle -- instead of sudden and fast. This affords ample time to put on and take off the necessary amount of rudder.

118

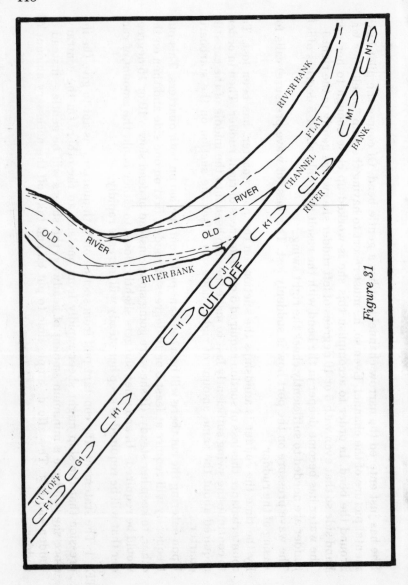

Figure 31

F1. Shortly after entering the cut the ship unavoidably gets closer to her starboard hand bank. This causes her to want to get away from it. This, also, is what we want her to do -- but not too fast.

G1. She swings gently to port against 10 degrees of right rudder.

H1. Then 15 degrees of right rudder enables her to steady up in the middle of the cut. (Of course various amounts of rudder -- both left and right -- will then be required to keep her steady.)

I1. She has been worked up slightly close to her port hand bank and is being held parallel to it with 10 degrees of left rudder.

J1. By easing the rudder to amidships the predominance of suction on the port quarter caused her to swing to starboard. But when her head gets beyond the point the wave pressure on the port bow is lost, the wave pressure on the starboard bow *increases*, and the suction pull on the port quarter *decreases*. This combination arrests the swing; and she would head for the open water but is prevented from doing so with right rudder.

K1. Ship is headed toward the bend.

L1. She is kept in the bend with about 25 degrees of right rudder. Then

M1. by having eased the rudder to amidships--while at L1--she starts swinging to port. However, almost immediately this swing must be checked (and soon afterwards stopped). Therefore the rudder now is put full right.

Naturally, for awhile the swing continues. As it (the swing) decreases the rudder accordingly is, only, eased--because the swing to port needs to continue just a trifle longer in order to get in a favorable position entering another CUT OFF (see Figure 32).

N1. She is in proper position to enter the CUT OFF (which is immediately ahead).
The pull from Suction on the starboard quarter has *decreased* in about the same proportion that the quantity of water on the port quarter has *increased*. Consequently she now readily answers her rudder.

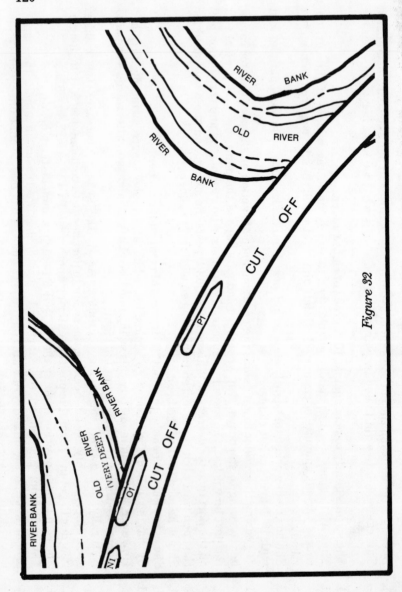

Figure 32

O1. It will require only about 5 degrees of left rudder to offset the wave pressure on the port bow because the ship's port quarter is abreast of deep open water. Therefore, it is free from the influence of suction.

NOTE: 2 This is an appropriate place to point out that bow-wave is not of as much consequence as the comments and illustrations might have seemed to imply. For example, even though the bow is close to the port bank it can be held in position with very little rudder because of the absence of suction.

For the sake of illustration it will be assumed the cut runs straight. In which case it will require about 10 degrees of left rudder -- instead of 5 -- to keep her steady. This is because a ship will conform to a bend with less rudder than is required to hold her parallel to a straight bank.

Possibly tests have never been made to determine the proportionate effect of bow-wave and (stern) suction as it pertains to a loaded (or nearly loaded) ship. However, years of observation have brought forth the conclusion that suction is, roughly, three times as effective as bow-wave. For example a sheer, caused by suction alone, that requires, say, 27 or 28 degrees of rudder can readily be broken by giving full (or 35 degrees) rudder. On the other hand, if bow-wave requires about 9 or 10 degrees of -- additional -- rudder, then the sheer cannot be broken.

P1. After the ship gets completely in the cut she will require about 20 degrees of left rudder to cause her to conform to the bend.

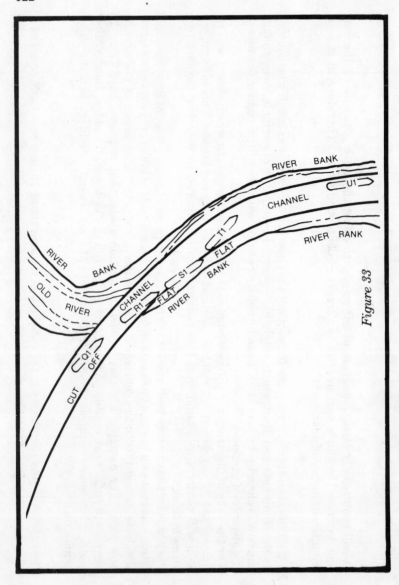

Figure 33

Q1. It is essential in order to prevent the ship from taking a run towards the open water—that is being approached on the port bow—to not only maintain the gently swing but increase it slightly. In order to accomplish this the rudder is eased, probably to amidships, shortly before the bow gets abreast of the point. Just after the easing of the rudder causes the swing to start accelerating, the loss of the wave pressure (on the port bow) would decrease the swing; however this is prevented by giving right rudder.

R1. Then sufficient additional right rudder is given to cause her to head a little more towards the bend.

S1. Because of the deepness of the water on the flat less suction is being created. Therefore when the rudder is eased to amidships she only starts swinging to port gently.

T1. Consequently she can easily be steadied up; then, at the proper time, be made to conform to the bend.

U1. The ship is being held close to her port hand bank in order to be prepared to make a very sharp swing to starboard.

NOTE: 3 In order to most successfully handle a ship under the foregoing condition it is important (except in the straight reaches) to cause her to develop a rhythm so that when one swing is completed—it is not too soon or too late*—it is at exactly the correct time and position to start the next one.

124

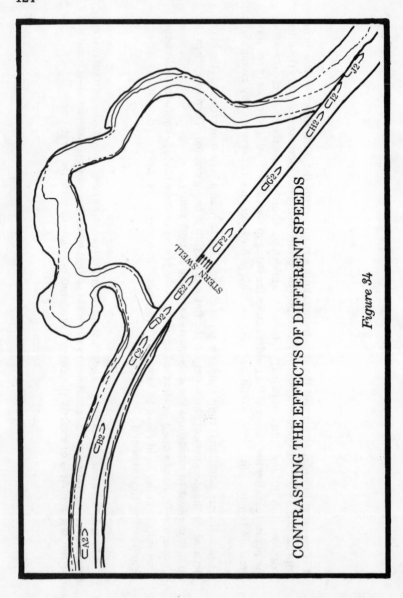

CONTRASTING THE EFFECTS OF DIFFERENT SPEEDS

Figure 34

Commentary: For the purpose of contrasting what can be the difference in the outcome when a ship proceeds with a minimum amount of headway and when she proceeds with slightly more speed, it will be presumed the ship that was being discussed, again, leaves the same dock with all conditions the same except that this time the engine is worked slow instead of dead slow.

A2. & B2. As far as can be detected only a normal amount of left rudder is required to check the swing to the right sufficiently to hold the ship the customary distance away from the bank.

C2. & D2. Also at these two positions only a normal amount of rudder seems to be required.

E2. However, upon entering the cut, from 10 to 15 degrees of rudder are needed. This is too much!

F2. Consequently, the engine's revolutions are reduced to dead slow. But almost immediately the stern swell overtakes and lifts the after portion of the ship enough to cause a sheer. To quickly get more rudder power, for the purpose of breaking the sheer before the head swings too far, the engine is worked half speed ahead. This breaks the sheer and enables her to be steadied up. As soon as this is accomplished the engine, again, is worked slow. Although she still can be kept under control the "kick" half speed ahead increases the headway slightly. Consequently it now requires a few more degrees of rudder to keep her steady.

NOTE: 4 In spite of the implication that excessive headway cannot be reduced, the only situation where this cannot be accomplished is with a motorship where the engine, already, is being worked as slowly as possible. Otherwise, by reducing the engine's speed, say, one or two revolutions at a time the headway can gradually be gotten off.

G2. It would be desirable to favor the port hand bank shortly before leaving the cut. However, this cannot be done since she is on the verge of going wild even while being held in the middle.

H2. As soon as the wave pressure on the port bow is lost the ship takes a sheer to port.

I2. Bow strikes shoal water.

J2. Ship is aground.

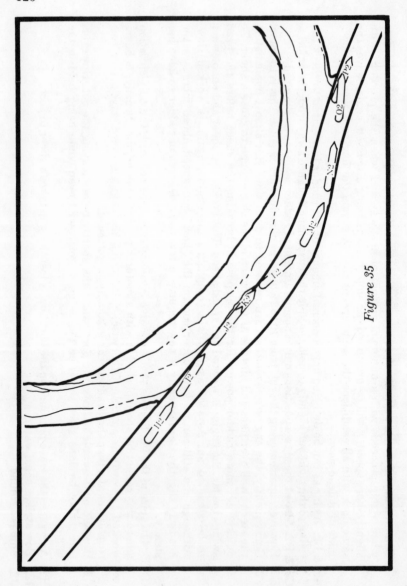

Figure 35

127

For the purpose of showing a different outcome we will revert to "H2".

H2.   As soon as the wave pressure on the port bow is lost the ship takes a run for the open water.

I2.   Bow strikes shoal water causing the ship to swing parallel to the edge of the channel.

J2.   (Instead of grounding) she drags along the edge of the channel.

K2.   By giving her full speed ahead and with full right rudder she suddenly frees heself and swings to "L 2".

L2.   When this happens -- before she can gather much headway -- the rudder is reversed to full left and the engine's speed is reduced to slow. Nevertheless she gets to (M2)

M2.   before wave pressure on the starboard bow enables full left rudder to cause her to swing to (N2).

N2.   As soon as the ship starts swinging away from the bank the rudder is put full full right. Nevertheless suction on the starboard quarter causes her to, momentarily, continue swinging to the left. Then she steadies up and begins, sluggishly, swinging to the right.

O2.   Although full right rudder enables the ship to enter the cut it cannot prevent her from striking the bank with her port bow. After which the rudder is put full left.

P2.   By the time this position is reached full left rudder was able to steady her up because the port quarter was free from suction.

Comment: It occasionally happens, when a ship is being handled in close quarters, that a minor mishap is developing. Nevertheless it would be poor judgment to try to prevent it, if by doing so, there would be a strong probability of bringing on a serious accident. Here is an example:

Between N2 and O2 if the ship had been allowed to swing slightly to port before heading for the cut she probably would have failed to enter it at all. Instead, she might have gone "head first" into the point!

128

SUCTION VERSUS
PITCH - OF - THE - PROPELLER

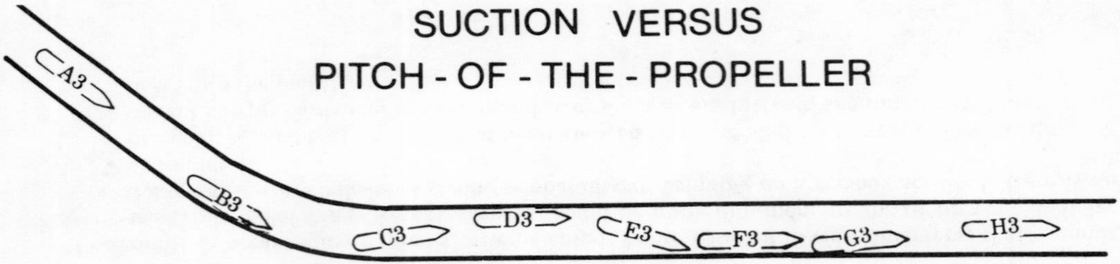

Figure 36

Commentary: This, again, is a "bad" handling ship. She is proceeding in the middle of the canal and is going dead slow speed ahead.

A3.   Ship is approaching a bend.

B3.   She, properly, is "keeping in the bend" after having entered it.

C3.   After completing the bend it is found—too late—that she cannot be steadied up. It is "too late" because by the time the propeller could be working full speed astern the bow—best would be grazing the bank and glancing off. Therefore

D3.   with full right rudder and the engine continuing at dead slow ahead the ship has grazed the bank. She now is on the verge of running away from it. Consequently the rudder is reversed to full left—and the engine is continuing to be worked dead slow ahead.

E3.   Although the rudder is full left and the engine is working dead slow ahead it can be seen the ship will strike the bank. Nevertheless letting her do so is better than any alternative.

NOTE 5: The propeller should never be put in reverse motion unless there is a reasonable certainty the outcome will be favorable. (In this case, since the propeller is right handed, the ship probably would become jacked.)

F3.   The ship again strikes the bank and again glances off. But this time, the instant this begins happening, the engine is worked full speed astern. The action of the propeller does two things, simultaneously.

G3. The pitch of the propeller tries to pull the stern to port. However the suction, created by the propeller's revolutions, is stronger. Consequently the stern is drawn toward the starboard bank.

H3. As the ship slowly advances the effect of the pitch of the propeller—in trying to pull the stern to port—remains constant. On the other hand, as the ship advances, her stern gets farther away form the starboard bank—causing the suction to decrease. Eventually, the pitch of the propeller will predominate and begin pulling the stern to port.

As this starts happening—with the ship sill having some headway,—the engine is worked full ahead on full left rudder. This steadies the ship up. With this accomplished the engine again is worked dead slow speed ahead.

NOTE 6: When in reverse motion the pitch of the propeller has a great deal of effect in drawing the stern to port. But in forward motion (when a ship is loaded) the effect is only slight.

TIPS ON GETTING AWAY FROM BANK

If a ship has gotten so close to the bank that it requires, say, 30 degrees of rudder to offset the pull from suction, she must be gotten in the middle—if possible. "If possible" explains why this statement might be contradictory.

When a ship is very close to the bank the instant the rudder is eased, only slightly, she will start running for the opposite side. To brake this sheer will require much more rudder than had been needed to hold her steady. Possibly as much as 35 degrees. However, if—and when—the sheer is broken, she then can be steadied up with probably 27 or 28 degrees of rudder. This will indicate that the pull from suction had been weakened. Therefore, the next time the rudder is eased there will be less likelihood of the ship going wild.

Figure 37

EFFECT OF
OPEN WATER

Explanatory Note: The bridge's open width is 200'. The canal's original width, also was 200'. However, the canal's present width is 400'. In the vicinity of the bridge all vessels must navigate in only one half of the channel width. Consequently, through lack of use, the other half of the channel silted up several feet.

To better understand why the grounding occurred the reader is asked to draw this mental picture.

As the ship was approaching the bridge she, necessarily, made a swing to the left. After her bow was headed for the middle of the entrance the rudder was put full right in order to break the swing and steady her up. Nevertheless - in spite of full right rudder - her head continued swinging to the left.

This was because (1) with her starboard quarter close to the bank she was getting a strong pull from suction on that side. (2) Furthermore, with so much deep open water on the port side there was very little counteracting suction on the port quarter. (3) The starboard bow was encountering a powerful wedge of water from the bow wave which was forcing her head away from the bank. (4) This forcing (away from the starboard bank) was aggavated by the "inviting" pull of much deep open water on the port bow - which the ship naturally wanted to head for.

Result: Forward part of ship is aground in unused portion of canal.

132

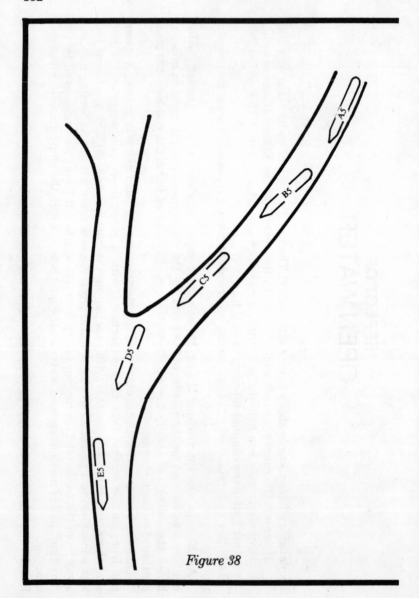

Figure 38

WHEN SUCTION IS STRONGER THAN RUDDER POWER

Commentary: When the SABINE-NECHES WATERWAY was opened to navigation in 1916 the juncture of the canals was found to be an extremely difficult problem, especially to get a loaded ship from the Sabine-Neches Canal into the Port Arthur Canal. Therefore the manner in which this problem was coped with will be discussed.

A5. Ship has been proceeding dead slow and has been gotten in position to swing toward her starboard bank.

B5. Ship, while still going dead slow is heading toward her starboard hand bank.

C5. The combination of dead slow speed and deep water alongside of the bulkhead (or bank) has enabled the ship to hold close alongside of it.
But now it is urgent to quickly build up as much suction as possible, without causing the ship to run away from the bank. Therefore full speed ahead is given; and just a little later full left rudder.

D5. The latter has caused the ship to start swinging heavily to port. However the help from suction is soon lost. When it is, the swing slackens considerably.

E5. Because of this loss of suction the swing decreased so much that the ship grazed the bank before the swing could be completed.

Remark: In many instances ships struck the banks heavily and occasionally there were groundings.

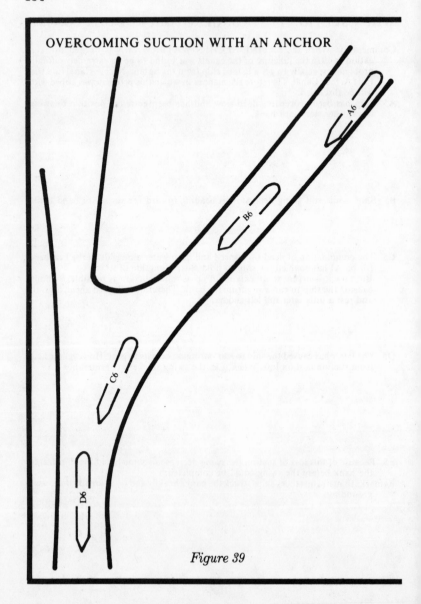

OVERCOMING SUCTION WITH AN ANCHOR

Figure 39

Commentary: To drop an anchor and drag it over the bottom when a ship has headway is considered to be such a hazardous undertaking that it is avoided if at all possible. However, so much difficulty was being experienced at the junction of the canals that the need seemed to justify the risk. Consequently the practice was started with confidence because after an anchor has been gotten on the bottom properly, and has only a short scope of chain it almost certainly can be dragged without difficulty.

A6. A bend has just been completed. As soon as this was accomplished the port side of the anchor windlass was locked and the port anchor was hove down until it took the bottom. This action has been delayed until right now so as to avoid the possibility of damage being caused by getting the anchor jammed between the port bow and the bank.

B6. With the windlass remaining locked, heave out until the anchor—which is already on the bottom—has several fathoms on chain. Leave the windlass locked but also set the brake firmly. A transformation has taken place! It is:

NOTE 8. When a ship that is underway is dragging an anchor on a short scope of chain the anchor will enable rudder power to overcome suction to such an extent that the ship can be held close to a bank—when she otherwise would sheer away from it.

C6. The ship was only going slow. When the anchor got on the bottom this reduced the speed a little more. Consequently because of the effect of the anchor the swing into the other canal was made with only 15 or 20 degrees of left rudder.

D6. Generally the anchor will have become so balled-up with mud that it can be hove up while the ship has headway. In case this is not possible—the headway will be so slight that—by stopping the engine it should quickly be killed. After which a kick astern will get the chain nearly up and down.

Remark: The foregoing procedure has been used many times without causing a mishap.

Commentary: If—she makes a sharp swing to port—the ship might strike a dock, instead of a soft mud bank, then special precaution will be taken to prevent this from happening. The illustration shows a loaded ship in the PORT ARTHUR CANAL—years ago when it was very narrow—approaching such a location.

A7. The ship is making dead slow speed and the port anchor is being dragged on a short scope of chain. The anchor was gotten on the bottom by backing it down, after which the windlass was left locked. Also, the brake was set firmly.

NOTE 9. When a loaded ship is in a narrow canal—no matter how slow the speed—if the engine is stopped, without having the anchor on the bottom, she almost certainly will take a sheer.

B7. The ship is steering perfectly—in spite of open water on the starboard side.

NOTE 10. When dragging only a short scope of chain the anchor is almost directly under the stem. From this location it controls the ship's steering nearly the same as hinges control the swinging of a door.

C7. There has been very little loss of headway. The reason, no doubt, is because the anchor has become balled-up with mud. Therefore, about another fathom of chain is paid out. The windlass is unlocked so as to be able to give more chain, quickly, if necessary. The engine is stopped, allowing the ship to head-reach.

D7. Upon arriving at this position the headway has not quite been killed. Consequently the brake is released and the chain paid out until the ship has gone ahead about a half ship length. After which the brake is set. This completely kills the headway. Therefore the engine is worked ahead slow with full left rudder.

E7. By the time the ship has swung to this position the anchor, fortunately, has dragged a little. "Fortunately" means the anchor does not have too firm a hold on the bottom. For this reason it, no doubt, can be hove up while the ship has headway.

USING AN ANCHOR AND CHAIN AS A SPRING LINE

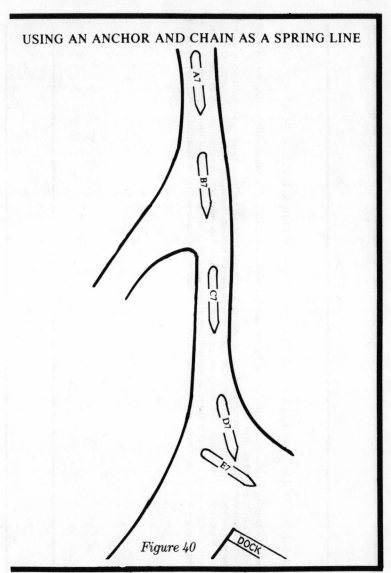

Figure 40

DOCK

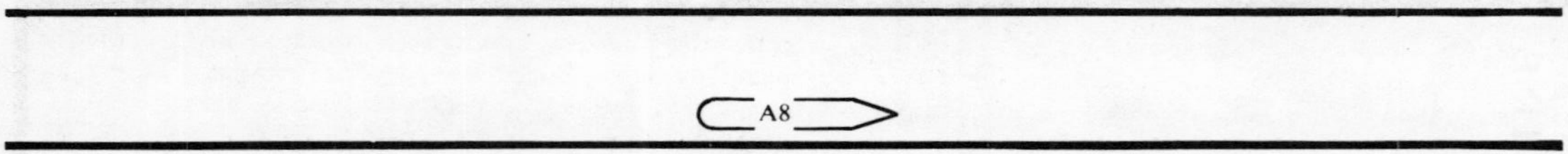

Figure 41

USING SUCTION IN LIEU OF A PROPELLER — WITH A TWIN — SCREW SHIP

Commentary: Steering a twin-screw ship when she has the canal to herself was discussed in Minimizing Suction With A Twin—Screw Ship (beginning on page 107).

A 8. Now assume she must prepare to meet and pass an approaching vessel. First, get her in the middle and—while doing so—stop the port propeller. Then let her headreach until time to giveway for the passing. During this interval a little more headway was lost. Which means that suction, also, has decreased somewhat. Consequently—with about an equal amount of mild suction on both quarters—when the port propeller is worked slow ahead she readily swings to starboard for the passing.

But, in case she won't steer with the propellers motionless, how she can be made to do so is explained in NOTE 9 on page 136.

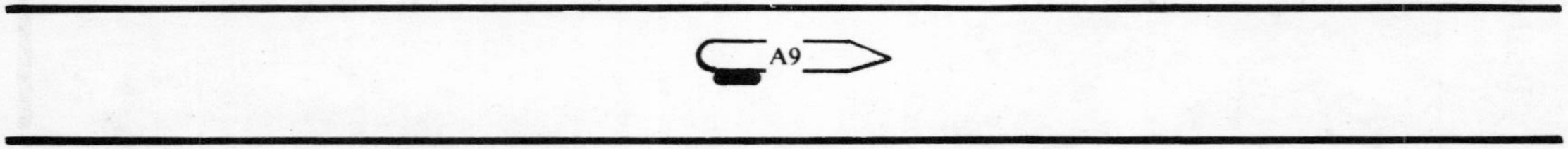

Figure 42

USING A TUG AS A PROPELLER AND AS AN EXTRA RUDDER WITH A TWIN —SCREW SHIP

Commentary: A very bad handling twin-screw ship generally can be kept under control by lashing up a tug on the quarter. (See 10. Lashing Up A Tug To Meet Different Conditions beginning on page 82.) When a tug is so used the ship's propeller on the tug's side should be kept motionless. (The reason for so doing is given in the first paragraph on page 109.)

In spite of the fact that the ship's propeller, on the side opposite to the tug, is--comparatively speaking--a great distance away from the bank the suction it creates should be about as strong as that which is created by the tug's (propeller) because it is smaller and is not as deep in the water.

NOTE 11: For the tug's rudder power to be the most effective the stern should extend slightly beyond that of the ship. However, if this were to be done there would not be enough of the ship's straight side for the tug to lash up to.

A 9. Ship has the tug lashed up on her starboard quarter.

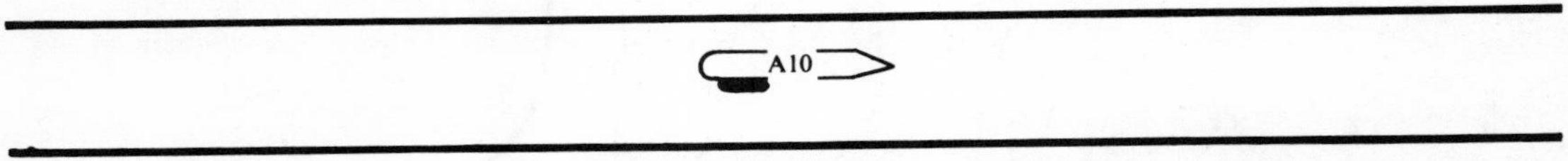

Figure 43

HANDLING A DEAD SHIP

Commentary: In case a twin-screw ship is so wild that both engines must be kept motionless she then will be thought of as a "dead ship". This term also will be used to apply to any ship that cannot use her own propulsion.

A10. How to lash a tug up to such a ship was dealt with in 10. Lashing Up A Tug To Meet Different Conditions, beginning on page 82.

To what was covered in the foregoing, this will be added:

A ship is the proper distance away from her near bank when the degree that she wants to run away from it is counterbalanced by the tug when her propeller is working full speed ahead and her rudder is amidships.

When this distance off the bank cannot be kept it is preferable for the ship to be held closer. In which case the tug must hold herself against the ship's side--thereby eliminating the possibility of her breaking adrift.

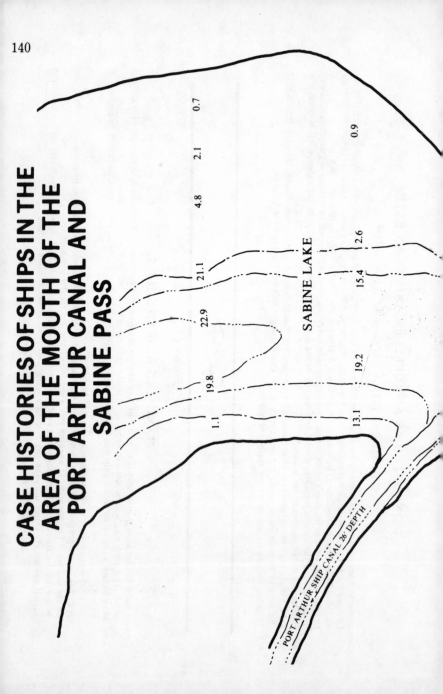

CASE HISTORIES OF SHIPS IN THE AREA OF THE MOUTH OF THE PORT ARTHUR CANAL AND SABINE PASS

SABINE LAKE

0.7

0.9

2.1

4.8

2.6

21.1

15.4

22.9

19.2

19.8

13.1

1.1

PORT ARTHUR SHIP CANAL 26' DEPTH

141

COMMENTARY: This overall portion of the Area adjacent to the Mouth of the Port Arthur Canal is for the purpose of showing, more clearly, why a strong flood tide is a problem for loaded outbound ships.

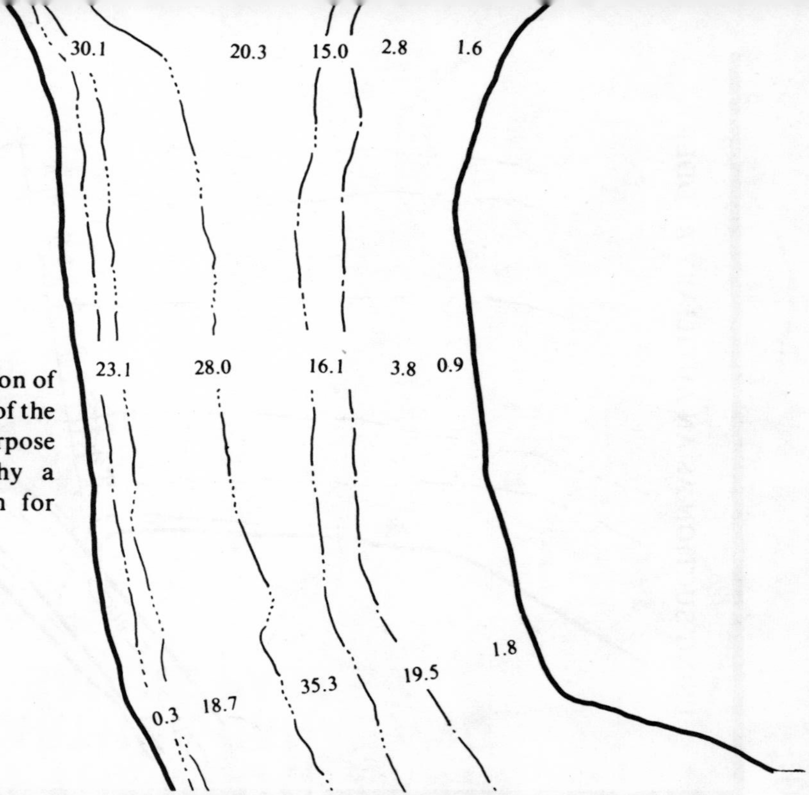

Figure 44

USING SUCTION AS AN AUXILIARY RUDDER

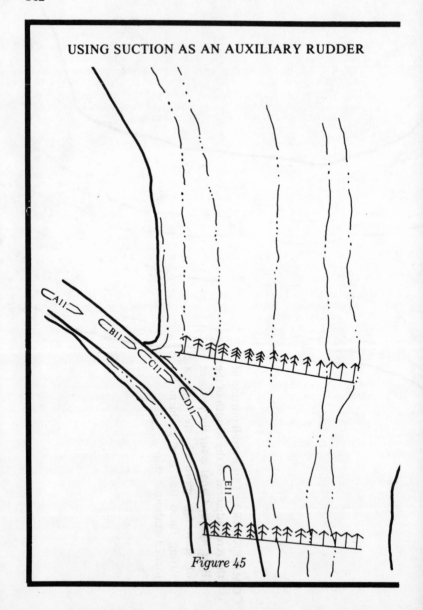

Figure 45

Commentary: When there is a strong flood tide in SABINE PASS it flows into SABINE LAKE, leaving the water in the CANAL slack--the same as it would be in a slip.

(There are conditions that cause the water in the CANAL to move in one direction or the other. However to simplify the illustration it will be assumed that during the discussion the water is slack.)

For the ship to get out of the CANAL into SABINE PASS when she must encounter a strong head tide requires exact handling. Long before approaching the mouth the ship must be "felt out" which is to say:

A11. Half speed has caused the headway gradually to decrease until 20 degrees of left rudder enables her to stay a little closer to her port hand bank. However, this is not close enough, therefore:

B11. Speed has been reduced to slow long enough to enable 15 degrees of left rudder to now hold her close enough to the bank.

C11. Being abreast of open water enables the ship to stay still closer to the edge of the channel with 15 degrees of left rudder.

D11. Just before the flood tide struck the starboard bow she was given full speed and the rudder was put full right. This (right rudder) helped by an "auxiliary rudder" in the form of suction on the port quarter--and full speed ahead--enabled the ship to continue making the swing.

E11. Ship has swung head to the tide.

HARM CAUSED BY SWINGING TOO SOON
(FIRST SITUATION)

Commentary: Ship is kept in the middle of the canal as she approaches the Mouth. Starting the swing too soon causes the ship to be harmed by ADVERSE SUCTION.

A12. Half speed has caused the headway to gradually decrease.

B12. Speed has been reduced to slow.

C12. Ship continues at slow speed.

D12. Ship was given full speed and full right rudder just before the head tide struck the starboard bow.

E12. After swinging slightly to starboard the head tide together with adverse suction on the starboard quarter caused her to sheer to port.

F12. Ship has become grounded.

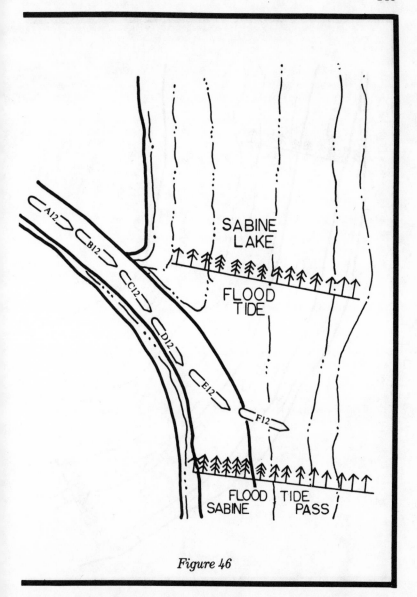

Figure 46

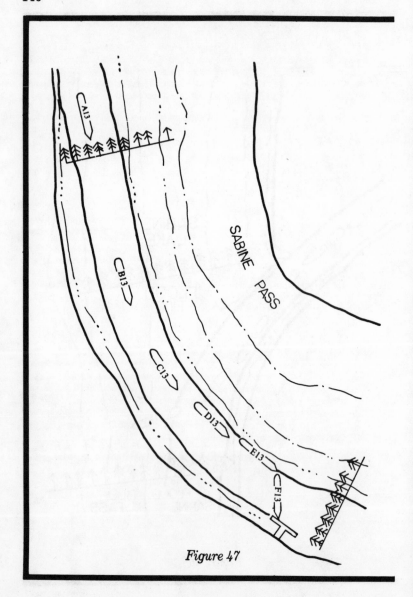

Figure 47

HARM CAUSED BY SWINGING TOO SOON
(SECOND SITUATION)

Commentary: Ship succeeded in getting out of the CANAL into SABINE PASS against a strong flood tide and is now at position A 13.

NOTE 12. Ship F 12 has been floated. Otherwise, good judgment would have dictated that Ship A 13 wait until the tide started to ebb before going out of the canal.

A13. Ship is in the middle of the channel and going full speed against a strong head tide. The intention is to hold the middle of the channel.

B13. Although the intention is to keep in the middle the natural inclination has caused the swing to be started a trifle too soon.

C13. When a ship is approaching a bend while stemming a strong head tide, in case the swing is started too soon, she gets the current slightly on the side; however this immediately starts setting her broadside, toward shoal water. Because of the narrowness of the channel it soon becomes necessary to give 15 or 20 degrees of left rudder in order to offset the pull from suction.

D13. Also, when "under the point" while stemming a strong head tide the tendency of the current is to set a ship towards it. Therefore she is now carrying 30 degrees of left rudder in order to be kept steady.

E13. Although the rudder is full left the ship takes a sheer to starboard which is aggravated by the strong flood tide.

F13. Strikes the dock!

148

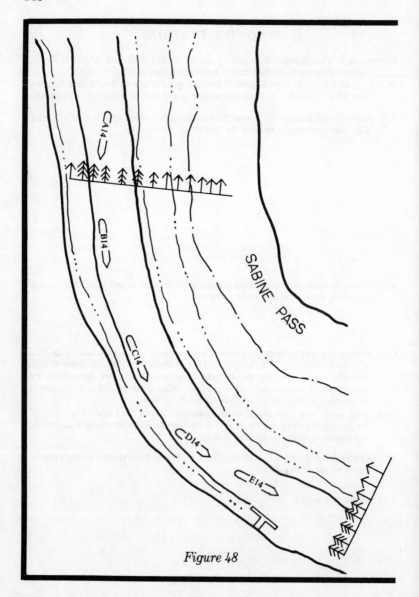

Figure 48

USING SUCTION AS A SAFEGUARD

Commentary: The aim of this--and the previous--situation is to demonstrate the importance of becoming "Suction Conscious" in order to handle ships more safely.

A14. Continuing to go full speed the ship had been swung slightly towards her starboard hand bank.

B14. Ship has been worked close enough to the bank that she can be held parallel to it with about 15 degrees of right rudder.

C14. Ship continues to be held close to the bank with about 15 degrees of right rudder.

D14. By easing the rudder slightly the ship is allowed to swing towards the middle.

E14. Ship is steadied up safely abreast of the dock.